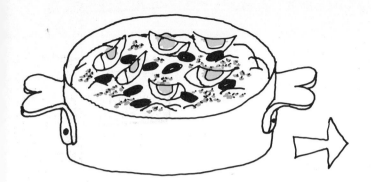

. . . wedges of hard-boiled eggs
with ripe olives . . . and a
sprinkling of finely chopped
fresh parsley . . . .

. . . a row of *thin lemon slices*
down the middle of the stew . . .
with finely chopped fresh
parsley . . . .

. . . a stew with vegetables, the
carrots and little white onions
showing . . . with freshly cooked
green peas strewn over at
the last minute. Good for a
browned or an unbrowned stew . . . .

. . . generous handfuls of watercress,
jammed into the side of the stew
at the last moment — it wilts
quickly — pimiento strips
down the middle . . . .

FOR GLORIOUS STEWS . . . .

GLORIOUS STEW

Glorious Stew

By DOROTHY IVENS

ILLUSTRATED BY THE AUTHOR

WITH WINE NOTES AND COMMENT
BY WILLIAM E. MASSEE

1817

HARPER & ROW, PUBLISHERS
NEW YORK, EVANSTON, AND LONDON

Grateful acknowledgment is made to the following for permission to use the material described below:

Hâché adapted from *The Art of Dutch Cooking* by C. Countess van Limburg Stirum. Copyright © 1961 by C. Countess van Limburg Stirum. Used with the permission of Doubleday & Co. Inc., and André Deutsch Ltd.

Pickled Sweet and Sour Vegetables, Five Fragrances Beef, Stewed Shin Beef adapted from *Jim Lee's Chinese Cookbook*. Copyright © 1968 by Jim Lee. Used with the permission of Harper & Row, Publishers.

Collops adapted from *The New York Times Cook Book*, edited by Craig Claiborne. Copyright © 1961 by Craig Claiborne. Used with the permission of Harper & Row, Publishers, and John Schaffner, Literary Agent.

Solianka and Äigo-Sau adapted from *James Beard's Fish Cookery* by James A. Beard. Copyright 1954 by James A. Beard. Used with the permission of Little, Brown and Co.

Blanquette d'Agneau à l'Ancienne adapted from *Paris Cuisine* by James A. Beard and Alexander Watt. Copyright 1952 by James A. Beard and Alexander Watt. Used with the permission of Little, Brown and Co.

Yogurt Khoreshe adapted from *The Art of Persian Cooking* by Forough Hekmat. Copyright © 1961 by Doubleday & Co., Inc. Used with the permission of Forough Hekmat.

Abbacchio alla Ciociara adapted from *The Pleasures of Italian Cooking* by Romeo Salta. Copyright © 1962 by Romeo Salta. Used with the permission of The Macmillan Company.

FIRST EDITION

LIBRARY OF CONGRESS CATALOG CARD NUMBER: 79–83601

Contents

Author's Note   15
Wines, Spirits, and Stews   by William E. Massee   21

BROWNED STEWS · BEEF

Basic Browned Beef Stew   31
   *Simple but flavorful beef stew, cooked with herbs and wine,
   vegetables added.*

Short-Rib Stew   33
   *Cut-up ribs, well relieved of fat by preliminary cooking,
   cooked in beef broth and wine vinegar, with marjoram, caraway seeds, and lemon rind.*

Hâché   35
   *Hâché means stewed meat in Dutch; this is a simple dish with
   beef, vinegar, Worcestershire, and cloves.*

Carbonnades Flamandes   37
   A classic Belgian stew of beef and onions, cooked in beer.

Beef with Sour Cream   39
   *Simple beef stew with herbs and wine finished with sour
   cream.*

Beef Stroganoff   41
   *A longer-cooking version of the old favorite, made with round
   steak; it has a touch of mustard and tomato paste, and is
   finished with sour cream and sherry.*

Ragoût de Boeuf Bordelais   44
French beef stew, with meat marinated and cooked in red Bordeaux, vegetables added.

Boeuf Bourguignon   46
French beef stew, flamed in Cognac, cooked in red Burgundy, finished with tiny white onions and mushrooms.

Boeuf à la Hongroise   49
Hungarian goulash, French style, with onions, paprika, thyme, parsley, and bay leaf, cooked in beef broth and tomato purée.

Carne all'Ungherese   51
Hungarian beef goulash, Italian style, with marjoram and grated lemon rind, as well as the usual onions, tomato paste, and paprika.

Manzo Garofanato   53
Italian beef stew, with cloves, nutmeg, cinnamon, and lots of garlic cooked in red wine and tomatoes. Celery, cooked separately, added at the end.

Stifado   55
Greek beef stew, with cinnamon, cloves, and allspice, and equal weight of beef and tiny white onions.

Yoghurt Khoreshe   57
Khoreshe is the Persian word for stew; this one is made with meatballs, highly spiced, finished with yoghurt.

Carbonada Criolla   59
South American beef and vegetable stew, sometimes with added fruit. May be served in a pumpkin.

Chili con Carne   62
Mexican beef stew made with cubed beef, onions, green peppers and kidney beans, and seasoned with cayenne, orégano, cumin, chili powder and paprika.

Stewed Shin Beef, Peking Style   64

Chinese beef stew with star anise, ginger, soy sauce, Sherry, sesame oil, and scallions. Fresh ginger and star anise are essential for this dish.

BROWNED STEWS · VEAL

Etuvée de Veau au Vin Blanc   67

A French dish of veal in white wine, with a garnish of mushrooms.

Veal Paprikash   69

A Hungarian goulash made with veal, green peppers, onions, paprika, and tomatoes, finished with sour cream. Hungarian paprika needed for this.

Stufatino   71

Veal stew, Florentine style; veal in slices rather than cubed, with bacon, rosemary, and garlic, cooked in white wine.

Ternera al Jerez   73

Spanish veal stew with cumin, with meat marinated and cooked in very dry Sherry.

BROWNED STEWS · LAMB

Navarin Printanier   76

French lamb stew with vegetables, theoretically spring vegetables.

Blanquette d'Agneau à l'Ancienne   79

French lamb stew, cooked in cream sauce and Madeira.

Abbacchio alla Ciociara   81

Italian lamb stew with ham, seasoned with a little rosemary, cooked in Cognac, green beans added.

Abbacchio alla Romana   83

Lamb stew Roman style, with sage, rosemary, and anchovies, cooked in white wine and vinegar.

Lamb Pilaf   85

Middle Eastern stew of lamb with fruit. Rice is cooked in it, and absorbs the liquid.

Lamb and Bean Khoreshe   88

Middle Eastern lamb stew with beans, cooked with parsley, scallions, spinach, and plenty of lemon.

Arni Prassa   90

Greek lamb stew with leeks, parsley, and dill, finished with eggs and lemon.

BROWNED STEWS · PORK

Brussels Pork Stew   93

Pork stew cooked in beer and beef broth, with rosemary, vegetables added, finished with a garnish of Brussels sprouts.

Szekely Gulyàs   95

Viennese pork stew with sauerkraut, cooked in white wine with bacon, paprika, tomatoes, caraway seeds, and juniper, sour cream added at the end.

Sweet and Pungent Pork   98

Chinese-style pork stew with vegetables and pickles, in a tomato sauce. Fresh ginger is essential.

Lion's Head   100

Chinese hand-chopped pork patties, seasoned with fresh ginger, soy sauce, scallions, and sherry, cooked in chicken broth; finished with Chinese cabbage or spinach.

BROWNED STEWS · CHICKEN

Coq au Vin Rouge   103

French chicken stew, flamed with Cognac, cooked in red wine.

Chicken Tarragon   106

French-style chicken, cooked in chicken broth and dry Vermouth with seasonings of thyme, parsley, bay leaf, and tarragon, finished with cream.

Mediterranean Chicken   108

South of France chicken in a smooth, strained, slightly piquant tomato sauce, with olives and mushrooms.

Chicken Cacciatore   111

Italian chicken hunter style, cooked in tomatoes and red wine, seasoned with garlic, basil, and orégano.

Chicken Paprikash   113

Hungarian chicken stew, cooked in chicken broth and white wine, with onions, paprika, caraway seeds, and tomato paste, finished with sour cream.

BROWNED STEWS • RABBIT

Lapin aux Prunes   115

Belgian rabbit stew with prunes, dried apples and raisins; the rabbit is marinated for 24 hours, cooked in red Bordeaux.

BROWNED STEWS • FISH

Sailors' Stew   118

Mediterranean salt-water fish stew, a variety of fish lightly browned and cooked in a well-seasoned, thickened white wine sauce.

BROWNED STEWS • OXTAILS

Ökörfarok Ragú   121

Hungarian oxtail stew with vegetables, cooked in tomatoes, beef broth, and a little red wine, with paprika and garlic.

BROWNED STEWS · VEGETABLE

Ratatouille I   124

South of France vegetable stew, mainly eggplant and zucchini, with onions, green peppers, garlic and tomatoes, seasoned with basil and orégano.

Ratatouille II   126

A drier version in a casserole.

UNBROWNED STEWS · BEEF

Basic Unbrowned Beef Stew   131

Boiled beef and vegetables.

Collops   133

English stew of thinly sliced beef, with anchovies, lemon, and capers, thickened with bread crumbs.

Pot-au-Feu   135

French boiled dinner of beef and vegetables.

Daube de Boeuf à la Provençale   138

French beef stew, with meat marinated and cooked in red wine, vegetables and herbs, finished with optional anchovies.

Russian Beef Borscht   141

Russian soup-stew of beef and beets made here into soup and stew.

Wienersaft Gulyàs   143

Viennese beef goulash, with marjoram, caraway seeds, lemon rind, the usual onions and paprika, cooked in water and tomato paste.

Puchero Criolla   145

South American boiled dinner of beef and vegetables, including squash and corn, with a side dish of garbanzo beans (chick peas) and chorizo (Spanish sausage).

Sweet and Sour Meatball Stew   148

    Beef meatball stew, cooked in tomato sauce, lemon juice, and a little cherry jam.

Five Fragrances Beef   149

    Chinese beef stew with fresh ginger, soy sauce, sesame oil, and the rare taste of five fragrances spice; cannot be done without these ingredients.

UNBROWNED STEWS · VEAL

Lemon Veal   152

    Veal stew with a little bacon, cooked in chicken broth and dry Vermouth, well seasoned with lemon, marjoram and cayenne; finished with artichoke hearts.

Blanquette de Veau   154

    French classic of family cooking, creamy veal stew, with tiny white onions and mushrooms; finished with egg yolks, cream, and lemon.

UNBROWNED STEWS · LAMB

Irish Stew   157

    New York version of the famous Irish stew of lamb, with onions, cabbage, leeks, thickened with potatoes.

Lamb Curry   159

    Indian lamb stew, with meat marinated and cooked in buttermilk, with the individual spices that go into curry powder, so hotness can be controlled.

UNBROWNED STEWS · PORK

Maiale Affogato   163

    Italian-style pork stew with rosemary, cooked with a mince of carrots, in white wine and chicken broth, separately cooked peppers added.

UNBROWNED STEWS · CHICKEN

Plain Old Chicken and Dumplings   166
Young chicken, cooked in home-made stock to make it more chickeny; with vegetables and dumplings.

Fricassee of Chicken   169
French chicken stew, cooked in thickened chicken broth and white wine, finished with egg yolks and cream, garnished with mushrooms.

Brunswick Stew   171
American chicken stew, with a little ham and veal, cooked in a rich sauce, with vegetables, including lima beans and corn, finished with Sherry.

UNBROWNED STEWS · FISH AND SEAFOOD

Äigo-Sau   174
Provençale fish stew with potatoes, onion, and tomatoes, served with a hot garlic sauce.

Bouillabaisse   176
Version of Marseilles fish and shellfish soup-stew, made with onions, garlic and tomatoes; seasoned with saffron, fennel, rosemary, and grated orange rind, as well as the ubiquitous thyme, parsley, and bay leaf.

New England Clam Chowder   179
Famous American soup-stew of clams, with crisp bits of salt pork or bacon, potatoes, and cream, with an optional dash of Cognac.

Manhattan Clam Chowder   180
New York version of the famous soup-stew of clams, with onions, celery, green peppers, carrots, potatoes, and tomatoes.

Creole Jambalaya   183
Southern United States dish of ham cooked with green pepper, onion, tomatoes, and water; rice added to absorb the liquid; raw shrimp cooked in with it all.

Solianka   185

> *Russian soup-stew of salmon, in fish stock and cooked-down
> tomatoes, with the addition of chopped dill pickles, chopped
> green and black olives, and capers.*

Seafare Stew   187

> *Scallops, shrimp and haddock in tomato purée, white wine,
> and fish stock, with saffron and a little hot pepper; raw clams
> added to open in the stew; licorice-flavored liqueur as final
> flourish.*

UNBROWNED STEWS • TRIPE

Portuguese Tripe   189

> *Tripe cooked separately, then cooked in veal stock with ham,
> white beans, tomatoes, carrots, onions, and essential Spanish
> sausage (chorizo). Takes a long time.*

UNBROWNED STEWS • OXTAILS

Oxtail Ragoût   193

> *Boiled stew of oxtails, with vegetables, cooked in water and
> tomato purée.*

UNBROWNED STEWS • VEGETABLE

Soupe au Pistou   196

> *French vegetable soup-stew with an added sauce of basil,
> garlic, cheese, and olive oil. Fresh basil if possible.*

Before, During, and After the Stew: Some Additional
Recipes   201

Sources   232

A Stew Glossary   235

Pronunciation Guide   250

Index   251

Author's Note

This cookbook came about through a chance remark of my husband's that, for all its fancy name, Boeuf Bourguignon was just a glorious stew. We began to make a list of dishes which could be called stews: Blanquette de Veau, Jambalaya, Beef Stroganoff, Lamb Curry. The list went on and on, and we soon realized that almost every country has its version of stew, and felt that this discovery was too good to keep to ourselves. Hence this book.

A stew by any name is a great boon to a gregarious cook. It can be made ahead, so that one can be with the guests up to the moment of serving, rather than in the kitchen, missing all the fun. With a salad and cheese course and fruit, and with lots of wine throughout, a stew can be the cornerstone of a long evening of convivial eating and drinking, which is the way we like to entertain. And a stew lends itself to buffet serving, which is a blessing for dining-room-less people. Most important of all, stews look, smell, and taste delectable.

What Is a Stew?

My definition of a stew is small pieces of something cooked in some kind of liquid, a nice elastic definition which permits the inclusion of everything from a chowder to Chili con Carne. While most of the recipes in this book are for main-course dishes, the definition of stew has in some cases been stretched to include a few dishes which might more properly be considered soups (although they are hearty enough for a main course) and some vegetable stews that require a main meat course.

It was easy to decide what to include in this book. I broke down my recipes into a basic stew format, and any dish that fit into the format could be considered a stew. From these, I picked those that I knew from experience tasted good and looked handsome. I paid some attention to geographical distribution in the recipes, although France is heavily represented simply because it has so many good stews. When I had a number of similar recipes, I sometimes chose to include several which revealed interesting differences in technique or seasoning. There are, for instance, several versions of Hungarian Goulash, each with its own distinct flavor, and each delicious in its own right. On the whole, however, I have tried for as much variety as possible in the main ingredients, seasonings, and cooking techniques. Beyond all these considerations, I included many dishes that were simply too delicious to leave out.

It was harder to decide what to omit. I left some stews out because the ingredients are too difficult to obtain. For instance, Cocido is certainly not thought of as fancy cooking in Spain, but it calls for things such as pigeon, and a pig's tail, ear, or snout—not easy to come by here.

I've tried many cassoulet recipes, but have never come across one that seems worth all that time and effort. Again, Choucroute Garnie is probably just as much of a stew as some I've included, but to me it is more of a steamed dish. I've left out many fish stews because I felt the ones given were sufficient to illustrate the basic principles; stews containing a lot of lobster are not included because a family allergy has prevented me from trying enough recipes enough times. Then there is Waterzooi, the famous Belgian chicken stew, which is finally so much like chicken fricassee that it seemed redundant to include it. And so it went. Actually, no single book could contain all the stews in the world, but this one, I feel, provides a good initial sampling.

How This Book Is Planned

The recipes are divided into two main sections, Browned Stews and Unbrowned Stews. I hope that this self-explanatory division, together with the listing of ingredients by category and in order of use, will make it easy to see how one recipe differs from another. In the introductions to each recipe we have provided suggestions for wines and other dishes to accompany the stew. Bowing to tradition in some cases, departing from it in others, we have tried to balance the meal to complement the stew, and also save the cook from too much last-minute activity in the kitchen.

At the back of the book there is a group of recipes for first courses, side dishes, salads, and desserts to serve with stews. Asterisks mark such dishes whenever they are referred to. Asterisks are also used following references to stews for which the recipe appears in this book.

The menus represent our way of life and entertaining, and can be condensed by those who have no desire to spend a whole evening eating and drinking. With crusty bread, a salad, and fruit, almost any stew in this book will make a marvelous meal for the most informal of occasions.

Finally, I should emphasize that the cooking time given at the head of each recipe is just that—how long the stew actually stews. It does not include preparation time, browning time, or reheating time. Furthermore, the cooking times are approximate, since it is impossible to be precise. They will vary, depending on such things as the toughness of a particular cut of meat or the idiosyncrasies of a particular oven. A stew is done when it is tender, whether it takes a shorter or longer time than that suggested.

A Note About Equipment

Flameproof ovenware casseroles, and baking dishes in a variety of sizes, are required in order to cook and serve stews properly. It is easier to cope with a stew if it is cooked in a large casserole, then transferred for serving to a smaller one in which the stew will not look lost.

Enameled ironware is the best kind of casserole to have, because such a casserole can be used for the bit of top-of-the-stove cooking that many of the recipes in the book require. Look for one with a good lid and ovenproof lid knobs and handles. It ought to be handsome enough to double as a serving dish which can be brought to the table.

You will find many uses for a cast-iron Dutch oven and it is a worthwhile investment. However, stews containing tomato in any form should not be cooked in it, since the iron seems to affect the taste of the tomatoes.

Earthenware or pottery casseroles are splendid for reheating stews in the oven, or for serving vessels. Since they cannot be used for top-of-the-stove cooking, however, they are less versatile than the enameled-iron kind.

Baking dishes come in an endless variety of shapes and sizes and materials. Since they rarely come with lids, they are used mainly for reheating (they can be sealed with foil for this purpose) and serving. You will find all sizes between 6 by 8 inches and 12 by 14 inches useful, since you will always have one that will just fit the stew. The stew should look piled up in a baking dish, rather than just *in* it.

The recipes for this book were tested with the following equipment, which might be regarded as a basic wardrobe of stew vessels:

Casseroles: 5½-quart, 4-quart, 2½-quart, 1½-quart. I could have used a 2-quart and perhaps one more 1½-quart casserole and a shallow 3-quart one for fish stews. But I managed, using regular saucepans and the spaghetti pot when necessary.

Dutch oven: 4-quart.

Rectangular baking dishes: 12 by 14 inches, 9 by 12 inches, 8 by 10 inches, 6½ by 8½ inches.

And in Conclusion

I should like to thank my long-suffering family: my son, John, age seventeen, who never knew whether he was going to have two or maybe three stews to try for dinner, or whether the entire kitchen would be full of manuscript, with no dinner at all to be had; my daughter, Cathy, a budding cook, who put her mind to some research for me when she had her fall wedding to think about.

And my husband, Bill Massee, who was deeply involved with the book, fussing over the recipe introductions and contributing the wine information. He has eaten stews, however glorious, beyond the call of duty, and what is more, as a cook with a limited repertoire, even tested some of the recipes with great success. In fact, he seemed to find the ones he tried particularly edible, an interesting development I wish I had discovered earlier in the game.

I should also like to thank a legion of brave friends, who ventured to try the stews cooked for the first time, who have tested recipes for me, and who have come over and helped me work out a word-of-mouth recipe. I am particularly grateful to Philip Hall, Esta Wilentz, Mary Gandall, and Joan Wilentz. I should also like to thank Mariusa Verbrugghe, who gave me much time on the telephone on the subject of South American stews, and who made the unforgettable remark, "We never put garbanzos <u>in</u> the puchero," which has become part of our lives.

Dorothy Ivens

New York
March, 1969

Wines, Spirits, and Stews

By WILLIAM E. MASSEE

A good wine—one without any unpleasant characteristics of smell or taste—adds overtones to a dish, whether it is used in the stewing liquid or as a marinade. Only the flavor remains, since the alcohol disappears in the first few minutes of cooking. It will evaporate even when simply added to a hot dish. Not only does wine flavor a stew, but its fruit acids tenderize tough fibers of meat and beans in the same way vinegar does.

"The better the wine the better the dish," cooks are fond of saying, but the subtleties of a great wine are lost in cooking. A better maxim is "The subtler the dish the better the wine." A gently cooked blanquette or a delicate sauce imparts more of a fine wine's savor than does a dish pungent with garlic or spices, which would call for a younger, cheaper, coarser wine.

The wine used in cooking is invariably a good one to serve with the dish; a stew made with Burgundy tastes best when served with a Burgundy. A wine you wouldn't want to drink is a wine you would be wasting your time using in cooking. The exception is a wine that has been opened for two or three days and has lost its freshness; it isn't pleasant to drink but is fine for cooking. Wines will keep for cooking purposes for perhaps a month (if corked and refrigerated). Champagne that has gone flat is marvelous in cooking.

Cooking wines are sold. They are unfit for cooking. They are generally ordinary wines to which salt or sugar has been added so that they are undrinkable. All their ordinariness comes out when they are used to make a dish. What every good cook needs is a bountiful supply of sound, well-made wines to be used freely—a good white, a good red, a dry Sherry and a sweet one, both sweet and dry Vermouths— that cost not much more than two dollars a bottle. Most recipes call for a cup or two of wine, a minor cost in a good dish, and what's left over can be used in another dish, or drunk.

To see how wines can change a dish, select a favorite recipe—let us say one calling for veal or chicken—making it first with red wine, then with white, then with Champagne or a good, dry sparkling wine from the Jura, the Savoie, California, or New York. Try the dish with a flowery white from Alsace or the other Rhine wine regions. Make a version using a red Bordeaux, a light Burgundy like Beaujolais, a fuller Burgundy like Beaune or Nuits-St.-Georges, or one of the Rhône reds.

Try the dish with a dry Vermouth or Sherry, cut half and half with water or stock. The dish will vary subtly with each wine.

When experimenting with recipes, the best wine to use is the simplest wine. A simple wine is young, usually a regional wine marketed as Bordeaux Rouge, Côte de Beaune Villages, Mountain Red, or some such broad category. It should not cost much more than two dollars a bottle. The European practice is to market wines under regional and district names, the very best wines carrying a vineyard name, as well. A Burgundy from the town of Volnay, for example, will be less expensive than a wine from this township that has a vineyard name on it, such as Volnay Caillerets.

Here is a list of good wines for the kitchen. American wines similar to European ones are listed wherever possible, and are then listed again in order of quality at the end of the sections. At the end of the listings are some added notes on brandies and other spirits that glorify a dish.

Red Wines (by region)

BURGUNDY The Pinot Noir grape produces all the great red Burgundies —from Chambertin to Pommard—but those marketed under vineyard names are generally too expensive for kitchen use when more than a cup is needed. Those with town names do very well for cooking, as do the fresh and fruity reds of southern Burgundy made with the Gamay grape—Beaujolais and Mâcon Rouge. California versions are excellent for cooking and drinking. Prices are for fair quality.

Over three dollars a bottle: Gevrey-Chambertin, Morey-St.-Denis, Chambolle-Musigny, Nuits-St.-Georges, Aloxe-Corton.

About three dollars: Beaune, Volnay, Pommard, Chassagne-Montrachet, Savigny-les-Beaune.

About two dollars: Monthélie, Santenay, Mercurey, Givry, Beaujolais, Mâcon Rouge, Pinot Noir, Gamay.

BORDEAUX The Cabernet Sauvignon is the great grape of Bordeaux, producing the most elegant of red wines, the greatest of which often take ten years to develop. The vineyards are called châteaux, and those wines bottled at the vineyards are called château bottlings, which is considered a guarantee of authenticity. The best of these were rated over a hundred years ago, and these vineyards are called classed growths. There is great demand for these wines of Bordeaux, and many of the wines now command premium prices. Price is a good criterion of selection, those costing under three dollars a bottle being generally excellent for cooking and drinking; they should be at least five years old. Those bearing regional names like St. Emilion are sometimes ready to drink within three years of vintage.

Over three dollars a bottle: Château bottlings of Médoc, Graves, St. Emilion, Pomerol.

About three dollars a bottle: Lesser château bottlings from the above districts, or wines of the Médoc townships of Margaux, St. Julien, St. Estèphe.

About two dollars a bottle: Wines bearing Bordeaux district names like St. Emilion, Pomerol, Graves, and Médoc.

RHÔNE
District names are used to identify the robust, full wines of the Rhône, which take four years to develop. Côtes du Rhône, a blend from scattered vineyards, is ready three years after the vintage, and has a hearty, rounded taste that makes it one of the best wines for regular drinking and cooking.

Over three dollars a bottle: Hermitage, Côte Rôtie.

About three dollars a bottle: Châteauneuf-du-Pape.

About two dollars a bottle: Côtes du Rhône.

OTHER REDS
Rosés are generally not used in cooking because they are too light; the best of them—Tavel and Grenache and Anjou —should be reserved for drinking.

Red wines, ranging from full to light, are made all over the world. The various regions for each country are listed in order of quality. Most cost between two and three dollars.

Italy: Barolo, Valtellina, Chianti, Bardolino, Valpolicella.

Spain: Rioja, Valdepeñas.

California: Zinfandel, Gamay Beaujolais, Pinot Noir, Cabernet Sauvignon, Mountain Red.

White Wines

BURGUNDY   The Chardonnay grape produces all the great dry white Burgundies—from Chablis to Pouilly-Fuissé. Those with vineyard names cost over three dollars a bottle and are too expensive to use when more than a cup or two is needed. Those bearing only district names or township names should cost under three dollars and can be used more freely, as can those made from the Pinot Blanc grape, planted in lesser vineyards. California versions are less full and dry, but are moderate in price.

Over three dollars a bottle: Chablis Grand Cru, Corton Charlemagne, Meursaults, and Montrachets with vineyard names, Pouilly-Fuissé.

About three dollars a bottle: Chablis Premier Cru, wines bearing the town names of Meursault, Puligny-Montrachet, Chassagne Montrachet, Santenay.

About two dollars a bottle: Chablis and Petit Chablis, Montagny, Rully, Mâcon; Pinot Chardonnay or Pinot Blanc from California.

BORDEAUX   Sauvignon Blanc and Sémillon grapes produce all the soft and flowery dry wines of the Graves district. These are reasonably priced for cooking when they cost less than three dollars a bottle. The rich, sweet wines of Sauternes are too sweet for most kitchen use. Marketed under grape names in California, the wines are dry and soft, reasonable for cooking when priced around two dollars.

Over three dollars a bottle: Graves wines bearing the name of a château.

About three dollars a bottle: Graves Supérieur, Bordeaux Blanc Supérieur.

About two dollars a bottle: Sauvignon Blanc, Sémillon, Graves Blanc, Bordeaux Blanc.

LOIRE The Sauvignon Blanc grape is called Blanc Fumé on the upper Loire, where it produces crisp, flowery wines. The Chenin Blanc grape produces soft and flowery wines in the middle Loire in California; both grape and wines are called White Pinot. The Folle Blanche grape produces fresh, sharp wines on the lower Loire and is used in the best of California Chablis.

Over three dollars a bottle: Pouilly-Fumé, Sancerre.

About three dollars a bottle: Pouilly-sur-Loire, Savennières, Vouvray.

About two dollars a bottle: Muscadet, White Pinot, Folle Blanche, California Chablis.

RHINE Riesling is the great Rhine grape, though its light and elegant wines are too expensive for the kitchen except when they bear only the town names of the Rheinpfalz, Rheinhessen, Rheingau, and Mosel regions. Traminer and Gewürztraminer are exceptional in Alsace, where wines are marketed under grape names, but these are almost too spicy for cooking. Sylvaner is soft and fruity, best in Alsace or Rheinhessen. California versions are reasonable for cooking. There the Riesling is called Johannisberger Riesling, and the Sylvaner is called "Riesling" or "Rhine Wine."

Over three dollars a bottle:

Mosel—principal towns are Piesporter, Bernkastler, Wehlener.

Rheingau—principal towns are Rüdesheimer, Hattenheimer, Johannisberger.

Rheinhessen—principal towns are Niersteiner, Oppenheimer.

Rheingau—principal towns are Rüdesheimer, Hatten-Ruppertsberger.

About three dollars a bottle: "Riesling," Johannisberger Riesling, Traminer.

About two dollars a bottle: Sylvaner, "Rhine Wine."

Most wines—sharp or soft, flowery or fruity—are marketed under district names and cost between two and three dollars, and it is always pleasant to serve a wine of the country with a dish of the country. District wines of the various countries are listed in order of excellence, although differences are not great.

Switzerland—Valais, Neuchâtel, Fendant.
Austria—Kremser, Gumpoldskirchener, Grinzinger.
Italy—Soave, Orvieto, Verdicchio.
Spain—Alella, Panadés.
California—Pinot Chardonnay, Pinot Blanc, Sauvignon Blanc, "Riesling," California Chablis, Mountain White.

Sherry, Port, Vermouth, etc.

Wines to which brandy has been added are called fortified wines. They vary from dry to sweet, and are admirable in dishes when used carefully. Herbs are added to make wines such as Vermouth, which are best used sparingly to give a dish a special quality.

Fino and Manzanilla Sherries—driest of all Sherries. A tablespoonful or so adds a special character. They are generally added as a finishing touch.
Amontillado Sherry—Nutty and lightly sweet, Amontillado rounds out the flavor of a dish, imparting fullness. It is the most popular Sherry for cooking.
Cream or Oloroso Sherry—Invariably sweet, adding richness to a dish, it should be used sparingly because of its sweetness.
Ruby Port—A little can be used to finish dishes with a sweet savor, particularly those with fruit, because it has a sweet and fruity taste.
Tawny Port—Older and softer than Ruby, it is good only

for delicate dishes. A tablespoonful is enough to round out a dish.

White Port—Although it is made from white grapes, white Port is coarser than other Ports and equally sweet. It can be used sparingly in dishes with some sweetness.

Marsala, Madeira, etc.—Generally sweet, these wines can be used like Port, to finish a dish and give it special character.

Vermouth—Dry Vermouth can be used as a substitute for white wine when it is cut half and half with water. A tablespoonful added to the cooking liquid imparts a special flavor. Sweet Vermouth can be used much like Port or cream Sherry.

Cognac and other spirits—Cognac, having a light, rounded flavor, is the best brandy to use for flaming or finishing a dish. Heavier brandies, like Armagnac or those from Spain, impart a heavier taste. Licorice-flavored spirits like Pernod, Ricard, Pec, and the Spanish Ojen have a remarkable sharpening and lightening effect on fish, chicken, and veal dishes, but they should be used sparingly—a tablespoonful at the end is enough for most stews. Gin brings out the flavor of stews with fruit and should be put in at the very end. Bourbon adds a graceful overtone to beef stews and to stews containing corn or beans. White alcohols like Kirsch add a tantalizing finish to dishes with cheese, grapes, or other fruit, and Calvados does remarkable things to dishes with apples. Except for flaming and finishing, spirits lend their character best to desserts, not to main dishes. American versions of these fortified or flavored wines usually serve well, although some may impart an undesirable off-taste to a dish. In any event, such wines and spirits should be used sparingly, for their tastes have a tendency to dominate.

Browned Stews

Beef

Basic Browned Beef Stew

for 4   about 2 hours

A basic browned stew would be one cooked in water and seasoned with salt and pepper. But it should be tasty as well, so this one has broth, red wine, and vegetables in it.

cook in:

3-4 qt.

serve in:

9" X 12"

The main thing to bear in mind about all stews cooked with vegetables is the timing. The vegetables should not be over-cooked; each should preserve its own texture and taste. The exceptions are the pot vegetables put in at the outset for flavor. These are often supposed to end as a purée; when just the flavor is wanted, they are strained out. This is a marvelous brown stew, a meal in itself. A red wine like Beaujolais or a California Mountain Red or Pinot Noir is a good accent. Like most stews, it is definite in taste and soft in texture, so a crisp first course of raw vegetables with a dip* would provide a contrast. A lettuce salad served after the stew in the French way, followed by soft Brie or Fontina with the last of the wine, could round out the meal, with fresh fruit of the season to top it off.

The vegetables in the stew may be varied according to pref-erence and availability. The potatoes may be left out en-tirely and a side dish of noodles, rice, Kasha,* Zesty New Potatoes* or dumplings substituted. The dumplings should be a kind that can be made apart from the stew, such as

Matzoh-Meal Dumplings* or Butter Dumplings,* since cooking dumplings in the stew would interfere with the cooking of the vegetables.

MEAT
2 pounds boneless beef shoulder or chuck fillet in 1½-inch cubes

Turn on oven to 325°. Dry meat in paper towels. It won't brown if it is wet.

FAT
1 tablespoon butter
1 tablespoon cooking oil, more if needed

In a heavy skillet, heat the butter and oil and carefully brown the beef pieces, a few at a time. If they are too close together they will not sear, and the juice will run out. As the pieces are done, remove them to a heavy, lidded flameproof casserole, with a very low flame under it.

THICKENING
2 tablespoons flour

Sprinkle flour on the meat in the casserole and stir with a wooden spoon until the flour is absorbed.

SEASONINGS
1 teaspoon salt
2 cloves garlic, chopped
½ teaspoon thyme
1 bay leaf
2 tablespoons finely chopped fresh parsley
5 or 6 grinds of the peppermill

Mash the garlic with the salt on a saucer, using a strong fork. Add to the casserole with the other seasonings.

LIQUIDS
1 cup dry red wine, Beaujolais or California Mountain Red
Canned beef broth, to barely cover (about 1 cup)
Hot water, if needed

Add the wine, allow stew to heat for 5 minutes, add the beef broth to barely cover. Bring to a simmer, cover, and place in the oven. Turn down to 300° or whatever temperature will just maintain the simmer.

Cook 1–1½ hours, or until beef is beginning to be tender. Check the stew occasionally to make sure it is not too dry. Add hot water to bring it back to its original level.

ADDED VEGETABLES AND SEASONINGS

4 medium carrots in
½-inch diagonal slices
2 medium onions cut in
8 wedges
4–6 medium potatoes,
halved

½ teaspoon salt
¼ teaspoon pepper

TO FINISH

1 package frozen peas,
cooked

GARNISH

¼ cup finely chopped fresh
parsley

Add the vegetables, sprinkle with salt and pepper. Cover and cook ¾ hour or until meat and vegetables are tender.

Tip pot, skim off fat. Check and correct seasoning.

For later serving, allow to cool with lid askew so the stew will not continue to cook in its own heat. Cover and refrigerate. Reheat by first bringing to room temperature, and then placing in a preheated 325° oven for 30–45 minutes or until stew is just bubbling and warmed through.

Add the peas.

Sprinkle parsley over all.

Short-Rib Stew

2/23/87 - Delicious - Incredibly Tender   for 6   1½–2½ hours to cook

cook in:

4 qt.

serve in:

9" x 12"

Bony but full of taste, this stew is a most presentable dish. The ribs are thoroughly browned to render their fat, which is drained off, then they are cooked for half an hour longer without liquid to render still more fat. They are then simmered in stock with onions, red wine vinegar, lemon rind, caraway, and herbs. Noodles with poppy seeds are a good accompaniment. A fruity wine like California Zinfandel or Mountain Red suits these short ribs. A fine first course would be black bean soup, with dark bread; a good salad would be lettuce with green peppers and black olives. Fresh Mixed Fruits* cut up and steeped in liqueur would be a cooling dessert.

MEAT
4 pounds lean short ribs
in 2-inch pieces

Turn on oven to 500°–550°.

Wipe the beef pieces with damp paper towels to remove bone splinters. Dry for browning; they won't brown if they are damp.

FAT
1 tablespoon oil

Oil a shallow roasting pan and place in the hot oven for 5 minutes. Put the pieces of beef in it, leaving them far enough apart so that the meat will brown rather than steam. Cook 10–15 minutes, turning once or twice to brown all sides. Turn oven down to 325°.

Transfer beef from roasting pan to a 4-quart Dutch oven. Cover and place in the oven for 30 minutes.

POT VEGETABLE
2 medium onions, chopped

Pour off fat from beef, add the onions, and stir and cook on top of the stove until onions are limp.

SEASONINGS
2 teaspoons salt
1 teaspoon pepper
½ teaspoon marjoram
1 teaspoon caraway seeds
1 bay leaf
Grated rind of 1 lemon

Add the seasonings.

LIQUIDS
3 cups canned beef broth
¼ cup wine vinegar

(2 cans)
12 oz

Add the liquid, stirring to blend seasonings and to detach any bits stuck to the bottom.

COLORING (optional)
1 tablespoon meat coloring, as unflavored as possible

Stir in meat coloring, if stew is not brown enough.

Cover and return to the oven. Cook 1–2 hours or until beef is fork tender. (The time is hard to predict because it depends on the quality of the meat and how much it has cooked during the browning.) Remove beef to a baking dish, keeping it warm. Skim fat off liquid.

THICKENING
3 tablespoons flour
¼ cup cold water

Make a smooth paste of flour and water, stir into liquid, and cook on top of the stove until it thickens, 2–3 minutes. Pour over beef in baking dish.

For later serving, cool, cover baking dish well with foil, and refrigerate. To reheat, place in preheated 325° oven for 30–45 minutes, or until stew is just bubbling and warmed through.

GARNISHES
½ pound mushrooms
2 tablespoons butter
10–12 cherry tomatoes

Sauté mushrooms in butter; sprinkle with salt and pepper; place on stew. Dip tomatoes briefly in hot water, peel, and scatter over stew. If cherry tomatoes are not available, use coarsely chopped pimientos for a touch of red.

Hâché

for 4   about 1½–2 hours to cook

cook in:

2½ qt.

serve in:

8" x 10"
9" x 12" with potatoes

A pleasant spiciness characterizes this simple stew, which is often served with black bread, boiled potatoes, and Red Cabbage.* A richer version could be made with beef stock in place of water, but be sparing with the salt if there is any in the stock.

Beer is the best thing to drink with this stew. A traditional Dutch preface to the meal is slices of Edam and Gouda cheese on dark bread, iced Genever gin served in tiny glasses and drunk neat, and something salty: slivers of ham, some herring, or dried beef (page 203). This might be followed by bowls of green pea soup with dollops of sour cream and sprinkled with chives—and more dark bread. For salad, a cool contrast would be thinly sliced cucumber dressed with oil and vinegar. A lemon sherbet with cookies or a bowl of fresh fruit is a light dessert, to be followed by chilled Kirsch.

MEAT
2 pounds round steak in 1-inch cubes

Heat oven to 325°.

Dry meat thoroughly in paper towels; it won't brown if it is wet.

FAT
2 tablespoons cooking oil, more if needed

Heat the oil in a skillet.

POT VEGETABLE
4 medium onions, chopped

Slowly cook the onions until they are limp and golden. With a slotted spoon, remove to a flameproof ovenware casserole that has a lid. In the same fat in the skillet carefully brown the meat, a few pieces at a time, moving them to the casserole as they are done.

THICKENING
2 tablespoons flour

Sprinkle the onions and meat with flour, stirring until the flour disappears.

SEASONINGS
2 tablespoons vinegar
2 bay leaves
5 cloves, broken
2 teaspoons salt
1 tablespoon Worcestershire sauce

Stir in seasonings.

LIQUID
2 cups hot water, more if needed

Add water barely to cover contents of the casserole, bring to a simmer, cover and place in oven at 300°, or whatever temperature will maintain a simmer. Cook 1½–2 hours. Check occasionally to make sure the liquid has not boiled away, adding hot water when necessary to keep stew barely covered. Check for doneness after 1½ hours. If meat is not fork tender, cook longer. Skim off fat; check seasoning.

ADDED VEGETABLES
4–6 large boiled potatoes, halved, or 8–10 small boiled potatoes

When the stew is done, pour it into a clean, larger casserole, or a 9-by-12-inch shallow baking dish. Add the potatoes, mixing carefully into the stew or arranging them around it.

To serve later, allow to cool, cover the casserole with its lid, or seal the baking dish well with foil, then refrigerate. To reheat, bring to room temperature. Place in a preheated 325° oven for about 30 minutes.

TO FINISH
¼ cup parsley

Sprinkle over stew.

Carbonnades Flamandes

1·25·87   for 6   1½–2½ hours to cook

cook in:

4-5 qt.

serve in:

9"x12"

This is a Flemish stew made with onions and beer, which reduce to make a marvelously rich sauce. The onions—traditionally equal in weight to the beef—will almost dissolve in the cooking. Red Cabbage and Apple,* regular cabbage with dill, or Braised Endive* is a good accompaniment.

Beer is excellent with the carbonnades, as is a four-year-old Burgundy like Nuits–St.-Georges or Monthélie. Consommé* can be served first. Sliced tomatoes and cucumbers dressed with oil and vinegar and sprinkled with chives make a pleasant course to precede the cheese, the choice of which could range from Gouda to Brie. Brandied peaches are a festive dessert, followed by Armagnac or Framboise.

MEAT
3¼ pounds beef rump or chuck roast

(used 2½ lbs of boneless beef ribs)

↓
not all that tender

Turn on oven to 325°. — Cooked in Le Creuset on top of stove

Buy a 3¼-pound roast, rump or chuck, trim fat, cut in ¾-inch slices and then into 2-by-4-inch pieces. Dry meat with paper towels. It won't brown if it is damp.

FAT
4 tablespoons cooking oil
2 slices bacon, diced

Bring oil to a sizzle in a heavy skillet. Brown the meat slices well on both sides, a few pieces at a time. As they are done remove them to a heavy, lidded flameproof casserole. Reduce heat and slowly cook the bacon pieces until they are barely crisp and not too brown. Remove to the casserole with a slotted spoon.

POT VEGETABLE
3 pounds medium onions, thinly sliced

Cook onions in the same skillet until limp and golden, not brown. Use more oil if needed. Remove the onions to the casserole.

LIQUIDS
1 cup canned beef broth
1 pint (2 cups) beer, more if needed later

Add beef broth and beer to casserole.

SWEETENING
2 teaspoons sugar

Stir in the sugar; it rounds out the taste.

SEASONINGS
2 tablespoons parsley, chopped
1 bay leaf
½ teaspoon thyme
2 teaspoons salt
4–5 grinds of the peppermill

Stir in seasonings.

Cover and cook in oven 1½–2½ hours, or until meat is tender. Chuck will take less time than rump. If necessary, add warm beer to keep stew barely covered during cooking.

Remove from the oven, degrease by tipping pot and skimming off fat. Check seasoning.

THICKENING
2 tablespoons cornstarch, blended with
3 tablespoons tarragon vinegar, or ⅛ teaspoon dried tarragon and 3 tablespoons cider vinegar

Carefully stir in the cornstarch mixture. Cook 10 minutes on top of the stove until the stew thickens.

  6–8 medium potatoes,
    boiled, halved, and
    peeled, or 12–14 whole
    new potatoes, boiled and
    peeled

GARNISH
  ½ cup finely chopped
    parsley

Turn into a clean warm casserole or baking dish, add hot potatoes, and serve. To serve later, allow to cool, cover the casserole with its lid or seal the baking dish with foil, and refrigerate.

To reheat, allow dish to come to room temperature and place in a preheated 325° oven for 30 minutes.

Sprinkle parsley over all.

Beef with Sour Cream

for 6   1½–2 hours to cook

There is no established category for a stew of this sort. It is not precisely a Stroganoff or a paprikash, but the kind of dish anybody might concoct after a bit of experience with stews. It is simple enough to become a standby in a busy household; flexible enough to be served with Kasha,* rice, Dumplings,* potatoes, Noodles,* or a White-Bean Casserole* and any number of vegetables. It is a beautiful beige color and tastes marvelous.

cook in:

3 qt.

serve in:

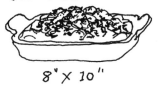

8" × 10"

Jambon Persillé* served with a fine white Burgundy—a Meursault or one of the Montrachets—makes an elegant first course. A light red Burgundy three or four years old, a Volnay or Beaune, or Santenay, is good with the stew. So is a salad of Boston lettuce and watercress. Follow it with some Brie or Camembert or Chèvre, and another good bottle of Burgundy. Pears in Red Wine* would make a fine dessert, with strong black coffee, served in small cups.

Turn on oven to 325°.

MEAT
  3 pounds cross rib or
    boned shoulder of beef
    in 1½-inch cubes

Dry meat on paper towels. It won't brown if it is damp.

FATS
　　2 tablespoons butter
　　2 tablespoons oil, more
　　　if needed

SEASONINGS
　　3 cloves garlic, chopped
　　2 teaspoons salt
　　1 bay leaf
　　½ teaspoon thyme
　　2 tablespoons finely
　　　chopped fresh parsley
　　1 tablespoon Worcester-
　　　shire sauce

THICKENING
　　2 tablespoons flour

LIQUIDS
　　2 cups dry red wine, Cali-
　　　fornia Mountain Red or
　　　Pinot Noir
　　Canned beef broth (hot)
　　　as needed barely to
　　　cover (1–2 cups)
　　Hot water, if needed

COLORING
　　2 teaspoons meat color-
　　　ing, as unflavored as
　　　possible

In a skillet, heat some of the butter and oil. Brown the meat well on all sides, a few pieces at a time, removing them to a lidded flameproof ovenware casserole as they are done. Use more butter and oil as needed.

Mash the garlic with the salt, on a saucer, using a strong fork, and add to the meat with other seasonings.

Sprinkle the flour on the beef, and stir over a low flame until the flour disappears.

Gradually add the wine; bring to a simmer; add beef broth; bring to a simmer again.

Add the coloring to insure a good brown color. Cover.

Place in oven, turning it down to 300° or whatever temperature will maintain a simmer. Cook 1½–2 hours or until beef is tender. If necessary, add hot water to keep the stew from sticking. The sauce can cook down a little, so the addition of the sour cream later will not make it too watery. The meat should show above the liquid. If there is too much liquid, remove some. Check seasoning. Skim off fat.

½–¾ cup sour cream

For immediate serving, slowly mix 1 cup stew liquid into the sour cream; stir the mixture into the stew. Allow the stew to come just to a simmer. Do not boil. Turn into a warm baking dish or a clean casserole if the working casserole looks messy.

For later serving, omit sour cream. Allow stew to cool, and cover casserole or wrap the baking dish well in foil. Refrigerate. To reheat bring to room temperature; place in a preheated 325° oven for 30–45 minutes. Stir in sour cream, after first mixing it with 1 cup of stew liquid. Put back in the oven for 5–10 minutes to warm through. Do not boil.

GARNISHES
¾ pound mushrooms
2 tablespoons butter
Salt and pepper
½ cup chopped parsley

Use whole button mushrooms or coarsely chopped larger ones. Sauté them in butter, sprinkle lightly with salt and pepper, then pile onto the stew. Sprinkle with finely chopped parsley.

Beef Stroganoff

for 4–6   1–1½ hours to cook

Beef Stroganoff was probably invented in Paris in the Gay Nineties, when hundreds of dishes were named after the royal or the famous. The dish is easy to make, its sauce is unctuous, and it keeps its savor for a long time when it is kept warm in a chafing dish.

Beef Stroganoff is usually made with the fillet, which means that the dish must be cooked at the last minute and served immediately. The round steak used in this recipe makes it possible to cook the stew ahead of time.

A light, young wine—a red Burgundy such as Santenay or a Pinot Noir from California—would serve this dish well.

cook in:

2½ qt.

serve in:

9"×12"

Stroganoff is rich, despite its fairly light taste, so a first course might have some piquancy: toast with caviar, for example, or something with anchovies, served with vodka, straight or in Martinis. A simple green salad would taste good with this dish, followed by a tray of sharp cheeses, perhaps Chèvre and blue. Pears served with chilled Poire, the Swiss distillation of the Williams pear, is a fine dessert, followed by coffee.

MEAT
    2 pounds round steak
    ½ inch thick

Turn on oven to 325°.

Trim fat off steak, cut steak in strips 1 by 2½ inches. Dry the pieces on paper towel. They won't brown if they are damp.

FATS
    2 tablespoons butter,
      more as needed
    2 tablespoons oil, more as
      needed

In a heavy skillet, heat the oil and butter.

POT VEGETABLE
    2 medium onions, chopped

Cook the onions until limp but not brown. Remove them to a heavy, lidded flameproof casserole.

In the same skillet, adding more oil and butter as needed, carefully brown the strips of beef, a few pieces at a time, removing them to the casserole as they are done. Keep a very low flame under the casserole.

THICKENING
    2 tablespoons flour

Sprinkle flour into the casserole, stirring until the flour disappears.

LIQUIDS
    1 can hot beef broth
      (about 2 cups)
    Hot water, if needed
      during cooking

Add the hot beef broth, stirring to incorporate flour and to detach any bits stuck on the bottom.

1 teaspoon salt
2 cloves garlic, chopped
½ teaspoon dry mustard
2 tablespoons tomato
  paste
5–6 grinds of the pepper-
  mill

On a saucer, mash together the salt and garlic. Mix the dry mustard with the tomato paste. Stir all into the stew. Sprinkle with pepper.

Bring to a simmer. Cover and place in the oven, turning it down to 300° or whatever temperature will just maintain the simmer. Cook 1–1½ hours or until fork tender. Add a little hot water during cooking if necessary to prevent sticking or burning. Tip casserole and skim off fat; check and correct seasoning.

For later serving, allow to cool with lid askew so the stew will not continue cooking in its own heat. When stew is cool, cover and refrigerate. To reheat, bring slowly to a simmer on the top of the stove.

TO FINISH

2 tablespoons medium-dry
  Sherry
¾ cup sour cream
½ pound broad noodles
2 teaspoons salt
Paprika

Stir in the Sherry and simmer 2–3 minutes. Add sour cream and heat, but do not allow to boil. Keep warm.

Cook noodles in 3 quarts boiling water and 2 teaspoons salt, or to taste. Drain, arrange in buttered baking dish or on serving platter. Turn stew onto bed of noodles. Return to oven for 15–20 minutes to heat through. Sprinkle with paprika.

GARNISHES

¾ pound mushrooms
  sautéed in 2 tablespoons
  butter, sprinkled with
  salt and pepper
¼ cup finely chopped fresh
  parsley

Use small whole mushrooms or coarsely sliced larger ones. Pile mushrooms on top, sprinkle with parsley.

cook in:

3 - 4 qt.

serve in:

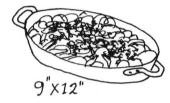

9"x12"

MEAT
3 pounds cross rib or
chuck fillet in 2-inch
cubes

The French word *ragoût* comes from *ragoûter,* meaning to restore or excite one's appetite. In this hearty version the meat is browned, after being marinated in a red Bordeaux, usually a regional from St. Emilion, Pomerol or the Médoc. The marinade is seasoned and becomes the cooking liquid, with the addition of stock.

The wine used in the stew is a good one to serve with it, although a château-bottled red at least five or six years old from St. Emilion or Graves would be more elegant, particularly if the wine is continued with a cheese course. Plain boiled rice is an excellent accompaniment although boiled potatoes are more traditional.

For a subtle change, try making this stew with a dry white Graves, omitting the green beans in the stew and serving peas as a side dish, instead. A white Graves served with this version should be three or four years old, and can be followed by an older red with the cheese. A green salad makes a nice transition between the two courses.

A light dessert like a Fruit Compote* suits this dish.

Heat oven to 325°.

MARINADE

1 cup dry red wine,
  Bordeaux Rouge
2 cloves garlic, minced
2 teaspoons salt
½ teaspoon freshly
  ground pepper
1 bay leaf
½ teaspoon thyme
2 tablespoons chopped
  parsley
2 or 3 whole cloves
1 tablespoon olive oil

In a nonmetallic bowl, combine the marinade ingredients. Add the meat, and allow to stand, stirring occasionally, for 2–3 hours, or refrigerate overnight. Drain, and reserve the liquid. Shake and brush off seasonings into the liquid. Dry the pieces of well-drained meat on paper towels. It won't brown if it is wet.

FAT

2–4 tablespoons olive oil

In a skillet, heat the oil. Brown the meat thoroughly in the hot fat, removing the pieces to a lidded flameproof casserole as they are done.

LIQUID

The marinade liquid
2 cups beef broth or just
  enough to nearly cover

Add liquids; they should not completely cover the meat. Bring to a boil, then turn down to a simmer and cook uncovered for about 15 minutes. Cover and place in the oven at 325°. Turn down to 300° or whatever temperature will maintain a simmer. Cook for 1½–2 hours or until meat is just tender.

COLORING (optional)

1 teaspoon meat coloring,
  as unflavored as possible

The stew will be a purply brown, which is a perfectly good color for a stew marinated in wine. But, for a little deeper color, add the meat coloring.

Check seasoning; degrease by tipping pot and skimming off the fat. The last bits can be removed by touching with a paper towel.

ADDED VEGETABLES
  12 small white onions
  4 medium carrots

Peel the onions and cut a small cross in the root end to keep them from separating. Scrape carrots; cut in 2-inch pieces and halve the thick ends to make them the same size as the small ends. Add the onions and carrots to the stew.

Cook 30–45 minutes more, until vegetables are tender.

For immediate serving, remove carefully to a clean warm casserole or warm baking dish.

For later serving, allow to cool, and cover the casserole or wrap the baking dish in foil. Reheat in a preheated 325° oven for 30–45 minutes after bringing dish to room temperature if it has been refrigerated.

TO FINISH
  12 mushrooms
  3 tablespoons butter
  ½ pound fresh green
    beans, cut in 2-inch
    pieces
  ½ cup boiling water
  ¼ teaspoon salt

Just before serving, lightly sauté the mushrooms in 2 tablespoons butter. Cook beans, covered, with the water, salt, and 1 tablespoon butter, for 10–12 minutes, until tender but still crisp. Drain beans and add both to stew.

GARNISH
  ¼ cup fresh parsley

Sprinkle with finely chopped parsley.

Boeuf Bourguignon

for 6   2–2¼ hours to cook

With Pot-au-Feu and Blanquette de Veau, Boeuf Bourguignon is one of the classic trio of *la cuisine bourgeoise,* French home cooking. The name should really be à la Bourguignonne—in the style of a Burgundy housewife—which refers to the sauce of red wine, bacon, mushrooms, and onion.

cook in:

3-4 qt.

serve in:

9" x 12"

It has to be cooked in red Burgundy; flaming with Cognac is probably a Parisian touch, marking the transition from provincial to bourgeois cooking. A Mediterranean friend used to marinate the beef overnight in red wine to cover, with a bouquet garni, and much more garlic than is called for here —six cloves. She added no stock, cooking the beef in its marinade. She didn't use any Cognac either. The stew ended up a rich dark purple and full of taste.

A first course in Paris bistros is often Oeufs Durs Mayonnaise,* but Consommé* is better. Boiled potatoes are the proper accompaniment, but rice or noodles are good, too. The wine for both stewing and drinking can be any red Burgundy, perhaps a Beaune or Côte de Beaune Villages. Salad can be a simple one of lettuce; the cheese should be the best you can find; and the dessert should be cool and light, such as sliced oranges in Kirsch, before Cognac.

MEAT
   3 pounds boned shoulder
     or chuck fillet of beef in
     2-inch cubes

Turn on oven to 450°.

Dry meat thoroughly on paper towels; it won't brown if it is damp.

FATS
   2 slices bacon, diced
   2 tablespoons olive oil,
     more if needed
   2 tablespoons butter,
     more if needed

In a skillet, cook the bacon in the hot oil and butter. When it is lightly browned, remove it with a slotted spoon to a heavy, lidded flameproof casserole. In the same skillet, brown the beef carefully on all sides, a few pieces at a time, removing them to the casserole as they are done. Turn on flame very low under the casserole.

THICKENING
   3 tablespoons flour

Sprinkle flour on the meat, toss gently, and cook until flour is absorbed. Place the casserole uncovered in the oven. Cook for 5 minutes, then toss the meat and cook 5 minutes more. This is to sear the meat thoroughly.

Return the casserole to the top of the stove. Turn oven down to 325°.

FLAMING
¼ cup Cognac

In a saucepan, warm the Cognac and ignite it with a match. Pour it, flaming, into the casserole, standing well back and shaking the casserole for a few seconds. Stop the flame by putting the lid on for a moment.

SEASONINGS
2 cloves garlic, chopped
2 teaspoons salt
6–8 grinds of the pepper-mill
½ teaspoon thyme
1 bay leaf
2 tablespoons finely chopped parsley

Mash the garlic with the salt. Remove casserole lid and add all the seasonings.

LIQUIDS
2 cups dry red Burgundy (Beaujolais or Côte de Beaune Villages), warmed
Warmed beef broth to barely cover (1–2 cups, more if needed)
Hot water, if needed

Warm the wine and pour in. Add warm stock to barely cover. Bring to a simmer on top of the stove. Cover casserole and place in 325° oven. Turn down to 300° or whatever temperature will maintain a simmer. Cook for about 1½ hours, or until meat is nearly tender. Check during cooking to make sure liquid has not boiled away. Add hot water if needed.

Degrease by tipping pot and skimming off fat. Check seasoning.

ADDED VEGETABLES
1 pound mushrooms
24 small white onions
2–3 tablespoons butter
Salt and pepper

Try to get small mushrooms 1 inch or so in diameter; they stay firmer. Wipe clean with damp paper towel and trim stems. If they are large slice coarsely. Peel onions and make a small cross cut in the root end to prevent them from separating.

Lightly sauté the onions and mushrooms together in butter. Sprinkle with salt and pepper. Add them to stew. Cook ½–¾ hour longer, or until meat and vegetables are tender.

For immediate serving, turn stew into a clean warm casserole or warm baking dish. For later serving, allow to cool. Cover the casserole with its lid or the baking dish with foil.

To reheat, place in a preheated 325° oven for 30–45 minutes, or until stew is just bubbling, after allowing to come to room temperature if it has been refrigerated.

GARNISH
¼ cup finely chopped fresh
parsley

Sprinkle with parsley.

Boeuf à la Hongroise

for 6   1½–2 hours to cook

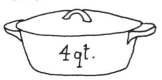

cook in:

4 qt.

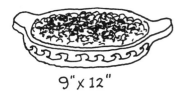

Serve in same, or:

9" x 12"

Paprika and onions impart a goulash character to this Frenchified stew, which is simple, hearty, and good. Traditionally, it would be served with noodles, but parsleyed boiled potatoes offer more of a contrast.

Any red wine complements this stew; try a light claret five or six years old, a Graves or St. Emilion. Oysters on the half shell, served with a white Graves, would be a fine first course, but Crabmeat in Aspic* would be even more elegant. A lettuce and watercress salad could follow, and lemon sherbet and Triple Sec would provide a refreshing conclusion.

MEAT

3 pounds boneless beef shoulder in 1–1½-inch cubes

FATS

2 tablespoons butter
2 tablespoons oil, more if needed

POT VEGETABLE

4 medium onions, coarsely chopped

SEASONINGS

2 tablespoons Hungarian paprika
2 teaspoons salt
2 garlic cloves, chopped

THICKENING

2 tablespoons flour

LIQUIDS

1 cup tomato purée
2 cups canned beef broth, or enough to barely cover

Turn on oven to 325°.

Trim fat from meat. Dry on paper towels, since it won't brown if it is damp.

In a heavy skillet, heat the butter and oil; slowly cook the onions until they are transparent but not brown. With a slotted spoon, remove them to a heavy, lidded flameproof casserole.

In the same skillet, brown the beef a few pieces at a time, using more oil if necessary. As they are done, remove the pieces to the casserole with onions.

Turn heat on very low under the casserole, sprinkle in the Hungarian paprika, stirring to blend. On a saucer mash together the salt and garlic with a strong fork; stir into the stew.

Sprinkle flour into casserole, a little at a time, stirring until it no longer appears white.

Add the liquid, stirring to blend with flour and seasonings and to dislodge anything stuck to the bottom.

ADDITIONAL SEASONINGS
¼ teaspoon freshly ground black pepper
½ teaspoon thyme
1 bay leaf
¼ cup finely chopped fresh parsley

Add the rest of the seasonings, bring stew to a simmer, cover, and place in the oven at 325°. Turn down to 300° or whatever temperature will just maintain the simmer.

Cook for 1½–2 hours, or until beef is fork tender, skim off fat, check and correct seasoning.

For later serving, cool with lid askew so the stew will not continue cooking in its own heat. When thoroughly cool, refrigerate. To reheat, bring to room temperature, place in a preheated 325° oven for 30–45 minutes or until stew is just bubbling and warmed through.

GARNISHES
1 green pepper in strips
2 pimientos in strips

Lightly sauté the green peppers in 2 tablespoons butter until they are just tender but still bright green. Scatter over the stew. Strew pimiento strips over all.

Carne all' Ungherese

for 4   1½–2 hours

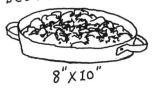

cook in:

2 ½ qt.

serve in:

8" X 10"

Hungarian goulash, Italian style, is tasty and not as heavy as you might expect—partly because of the grating of lemon rind, which has a lightening effect. Serve it with noodles to preserve the Hungarian touch, but garnish it with pimientos, green peppers, and black olives to give it the proper Italian bravura.

A light red Italian wine—a Teroldego or Santa Maddalena —complements this goulash, although a more full-bodied Hungarian red wine like Egri Bikaver would be an interesting alternative. The same wine can be served with the first course of Antipasto* and with Italian cheeses after the salad. Zabaglione or pears with cheese would be a pleasant dessert, followed by coffee and Strega.

MEAT
2 pounds cross-rib or
boned shoulder of beef
in 1-inch cubes

Turn oven on to 325°.

Dry meat carefully on paper towels. It must be dry to brown.

FAT
3 tablespoons olive oil,
more if needed

Heat the oil in a skillet. Brown the meat in the skillet carefully, a few pieces at a time. As they are done, remove the pieces to a flameproof casserole which has a lid.

POT VEGETABLE
2 medium onions, chopped

Cook the onions in the same skillet until golden and limp. Add onions to the meat in the casserole.

THICKENING
2 tablespoons flour

Sprinkle flour on the meat and onions; turn heat on very low under casserole; stir until flour disappears.

SEASONINGS
3 garlic cloves, chopped
1 teaspoon salt
1 teaspoon marjoram
1 tablespoon Hungarian
paprika
2 tablespoons tomato
paste
Rind of 1 lemon, finely
chopped

On a saucer, mash the garlic with the salt, using a strong fork. Stir in with the rest of the seasonings and cook on lowest heat for another 3 minutes.

LIQUIDS
2–3 cups hot beef broth,
enough to barely cover
meat
Hot water, if needed

Add the hot beef broth, stirring well. Cover and place in a 325° oven. Turn down to 300° or whatever temperature will maintain a simmer.

Cook about 1½–2 hours, checking the liquid occasionally, and adding hot water, ½ cup at a time, if needed to keep meat barely covered. Cook until meat is fork tender. Tip pot, skim off fat, check seasoning.

For later serving, cool and cover.

TO FINISH
1 green pepper, in strips
1 tablespoon olive oil
2 pimientos, in strips
10–12 black olives

Lightly sauté the green pepper in the olive oil, and scatter it over the stew, with the pimientos and olives.

To reheat: Place the covered casserole (or baking dish well covered with foil) in a preheated 325° oven for about 30–45 minutes or until stew is just bubbling. If it has been refrigerated, bring to room temperature before placing in oven.

Manzo Garofanato

for 4   1¾–2¼ hours to cook

cook in:

2½ qt.

Serve in:

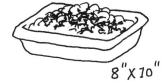

8" x 10"

The Romans used the spices of the East to enrich their foods. The cloves and other spices used in this beef stew do not end up tasting too much of themselves in the finished version. Fettuccine with butter and Parmesan is the perfect accompaniment, along with fresh peas or artichoke hearts.

The first course might be an antipasto, which would include salami and radishes, pickled peppers and anchovies, ripe and green olives, scallions and celery, strips of pimiento, and some slices of soft Italian cheese. White Frascati goes well with this, but if you plan to serve a Chianti or Valpolicella with the stew, you might start with the red wine right away.

A salad course is hardly necessary because the dish is so hearty and the antipasto so filling. Dessert might be pears or apples. Strega or Fior d'Alpi would taste good with the coffee. Hearty souls might cry for Grappa, the distillate of the cake of grape pulp left in the press after the wine has been squeezed out. Grappa is supposed to offend delicate feminine senses, but its leathery taste is just right after this stew.

MEAT
2 pounds boneless beef shoulder or cross rib in 1-inch cubes

FAT
3 tablespoons olive oil, more if needed

SEASONINGS
3 cloves garlic, chopped
1 teaspoon salt
6 cloves, broken up
¼ teaspoon freshly ground black pepper
¼ teaspoon cinnamon
⅛ teaspoon nutmeg
2 tablespoons chopped parsley
⅛ teaspoon allspice

POT VEGETABLES
3 large ripe tomatoes, peeled, cut in quarters, or 1-pound can undrained Italian tomatoes

LIQUIDS
½ cup red wine, Chianti or Bardolino
Water if needed to barely cover

ADDED VEGETABLE
2 cups celery, sliced

Heat oven to 325°.

Dry the meat with paper towels so that it will brown.

In a skillet heat the oil and brown the cubes of beef carefully, a few at a time, removing them when done to an ovenproof casserole that has a lid.

Mash the garlic and salt together on a saucer, using a strong fork. Add to the casserole with the rest of the seasonings.

Add the tomatoes coarsely chopped.

Add the wine, and water if needed; cover the casserole and place in oven at 325°. Turn down to 300° or whatever temperature will just maintain a simmer. Cook 1½–2 hours. Check occasionally during cooking. If the liquid cooks down too much, add hot water, ½ cup at a time.

When meat is tender, remove ½ cup liquid from the stew and put it in a saucepan with ½ cup hot water and the celery. Cook, covered, on a low flame until the celery is tender (10–15 minutes). Add to stew. Skim off fat; check seasoning.

For immediate serving, turn into a clean warm casserole or warm baking dish. For serving later, allow to cool; cover the casserole with its lid or the baking dish with foil.

To reheat, place in a 325° oven for 30 minutes, after allowing the refrigerated dish to return to room temperature.

GARNISHES
10–12 black olives
2 whole pimientos, chopped

Strew the olives and pimientos over the stew.

Stifado

cook in:

4–5 qt.

serve in:

9" X 12"

for 6   2–2½ hours to cook

This Greek beef ragoût with clove and cinnamon calls for equal weights of white onions and beef. Versions of this stew spread around the Mediterranean to become *stufatino* in Italy, *estofada* in Spain, *estouffade* or *étuvée* in France. All of them are supposed to be cooked slowly in a pot with a tight-fitting lid, with little or no liquid. Most such stews have rich sauces; if the onions are small enough, they end up like a purée, flavored with wine and spices. The stew is so hearty that only rice and a simple salad need go with it.

A full wine is demanded by this stew—a Châteauneuf-du-Pape or Hermitage from the Rhône, five or six years old—and the lightest of first courses, perhaps Jellied Chicken Consommé* with a squeeze of lemon. Bread and Greek Feta cheese are marvelous with the last of the wine. Fresh fruit is the best dessert, but if you omit the cheese course there may be room for that glorious Greek pastry, baklava, and strong black coffee with Raki or brandy.

MEAT

3 pounds boneless shoulder or top round of beef, in 2-inch cubes

FATS

2 tablespoons butter
2 tablespoons olive oil, more if needed

LIQUIDS

1 cup dry red wine, Côtes du Rhône Rouge
Hot water, if needed

POT VEGETABLES

2 cups Italian-style canned tomatoes, drained

SEASONINGS

2 cloves garlic, chopped
2 teaspoons salt
4 whole cloves, broken
½ teaspoon cinnamon
½ teaspoon ground allspice
1 bay leaf
3 or 4 grinds of the peppermill
2 tablespoons chopped parsley
2 tablespoons tomato paste

Turn on oven to 325°.

Dry meat on paper towels. It won't brown if it is wet.

In a skillet, heat the fat and brown the meat thoroughly on all sides, a few pieces at a time. As they are done remove them to a lidded flameproof casserole. Turn heat on very low under it.

Add the wine gradually, cover, and simmer 10 minutes.

Add tomatoes, stirring. Reserve tomato liquid to use in case stew gets too dry during cooking.

On a saucer mash together the garlic and salt, add the cloves to the mixture, mashing to break them up slightly. Stir into the stew with the other seasonings.

ADDED VEGETABLE
  3 pounds whole onions, as
    small as possible

In the skillet cook the onions slowly, stirring to coat them with oil, until they are lightly browned here and there. Do them in 3 or 4 batches, adding them to the casserole as they are done. Use more oil if necessary. Cover casserole and place in the oven at 325°. Turn down as low as possible to just maintain simmer. Cook 2–2½ hours or until meat is tender. Stir occasionally and check for dryness, adding a little tomato liquid or hot water if needed. Check seasoning and degrease by tipping casserole and skimming off fat. Remove to clean smaller casserole or baking dish if cooking vessel looks messy.

For serving later, cool with lid askew; when thoroughly cool, cover and refrigerate. To reheat, allow casserole to come to room temperature, then place in a preheated 325° oven for 30–45 minutes or until stew is just bubbling.

GARNISHES
  ½ cup finely chopped fresh
    parsley
  10–12 Greek olives

Sprinkle the parsley and olives over the stew.

Yoghurt Khoreshe

for 4   about 35 minutes to cook

cook in:

2½ qt.

Ladies who, in ancient legends, tempted lovers with choice viands made beguiling with spices of the Orient might very well have served Yoghurt Khoreshe. Certainly the dish is more than a thousand years old. Khoreshe means stew, and there are hundreds of versions, carried around the world by traders. The yoghurt gives the khoreshe a light and fresh taste, in contrast to the richness of the exotic seasonings in the meat.

Serve in:

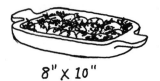

8" X 10"

Saffron Rice,* a pilaf, a Risotto,* or an Indian rice dish with raisins and pine nuts is the khoreshe's proper companion. A bountiful vegetable salad would be a good accompaniment, and while the Persians would probably serve tea, beer is better suited to our tastes. The French might serve cold Ratatouille* and slices of garlic sausage for a first course, along with a bottle of Beaujolais, and follow the stew with a tossed green salad, some goat cheese, and fruit tarts. In the Near East, a custard, ices, or a melon would be a more likely dessert.

MEATBALLS
 1½ pounds ground chuck
 1 teaspoon salt
 ½ teaspoon black pepper
 ½ teaspoon turmeric

Mix the ground meat with the seasoning, using your hands to spread the seasoning evenly through the meat. Form into 1-inch balls.

FATS
 2 tablespoons butter
 2 tablespoons oil, more if necessary

In a skillet, heat the butter and oil. Carefully brown the meatballs on all sides. As they are done remove them to a heavy, lidded flameproof casserole.

POT VEGETABLE
 1 medium onion, finely minced

In the skillet, cook the onion until it is transparent. Remove to the casserole with a slotted spoon. Turn heat on very low under the casserole.

SEASONINGS
 2 teaspoons curry powder
 6 whole cloves, broken
 1 teaspoon ground cardamom

Mix the seasonings together; sprinkle over the contents of the casserole, mixing well.

LIQUID
 1 cup hot water

Add the hot water; stir carefully to detach anything stuck on the bottom of the casserole. Bring to a simmer, then cover and simmer 35 minutes. Tip pot and skim off fat.

For later serving, cool and refrigerate. To reheat, bring slowly to a simmer after removing any hardened fat from the surface.

TO FINISH
 1 cup of plain yoghurt

Stir in the yoghurt. Cook, uncovered, for about 5 minutes, until yoghurt is hot but not boiling.

GARNISHES
 ¼ cup finely chopped fresh
  parsley

Sprinkle pomegranate seeds on the Khoreshe (if desired) or parsley.

Note: If stew curdles, cool ⅔ cup sauce, mix with 2 tablespoons flour. Mix well and cook, stirring, 1 or 2 minutes until thick and smooth. Stir into hot stew.

for 6–8   1½–2 hours for stew to cook
                ¾–1 hour for the pumpkin

Carbonada Criolla

cook in:

4 qt.

Serve in: same

or 9"–10" pumpkin

This South American beef stew can be served in a pumpkin, which keeps the stew hot and which looks marvelous. The pumpkin is baked separately, then the stew is put in. Corn and squash are essential, and some of the pumpkin is scooped out with each serving, these native vegetables contrasting admirably with the dark richness of the stew. Many recipes call for leaving the corn on the cob, which is cut into 1-inch pieces. This looks pretty, but kernels off the cob are easier to eat. The stew can also be divided between two small pumpkins, or can be served in individual ones, which would bake in less time than the hour required for the big one. It can also be served in a casserole.

This is a hearty stew, even though there are no potatoes in it, but pâté or ham with melon is a good first course. Nothing else need be served with the stew except good French bread, and perhaps some stewed or spiced fruits or relishes. Some recipes call for putting peeled peach halves in the stew for the last five minutes of cooking, but this makes the stew too sweet for most tastes.

A red Bordeaux—perhaps a five- or six-year-old St. Emilion or Pomerol—could be served. A dry but flowery white wine like a Riesling or Sylvaner is also good with this stew, because of the squash and pumpkin, and particularly if fruit accompanies the Carbonada. A salad seems redundant, although some people enjoy the crisp accent of sliced endive or celery.

The traditional dessert of the Argentine is creamed quince, Dulce de Membrillo, served with Bel Paese or Münster cheese and glasses of Ruby or Tawny Port. But the Brazilian favorite, guava paste, is much easier to find; serve it with cream cheese and crackers. Coffee should be strong and black, served with Spanish brandy, or with an Armagnac or Calvados.

MEAT
 3 pounds boned shoulder of beef, in ¾-inch cubes

Turn on oven to 325°.

Dry the meat thoroughly. It won't brown if it is damp.

POT VEGETABLES
 2 cups chopped onions
 2 cups chopped green peppers

FATS
 2 tablespoons olive oil, more if needed
 2 tablespoons butter, more if needed

In a heavy skillet, heat the fat and slowly cook the onions and peppers until they are limp but not brown. With a slotted spoon, remove them to a heavy, lidded flameproof casserole. In the same skillet, brown the pieces of beef, a few at a time, and add them to the casserole. Use more butter and oil if necessary.

SEASONINGS
2 teaspoons salt
3 or 4 grinds of the
   peppermill
1 bay leaf
½ teaspoon thyme
1 tablespoon tomato paste
2 garlic cloves, minced

LIQUIDS
½ cup dry red wine
2 cups canned beef broth
   or enough to barely
   cover

ADDED VEGETABLES
2 cups yellow squash in
   large cubes, about 1 inch
2 cups fresh green beans,
   cut in two
2 cups carrots in ½-inch
   dice
1 one-pound can tomatoes,
   drained and chopped
   coarsely
1 can corn kernels,
   drained, or 1 package
   frozen

TO FINISH (optional)
1 pumpkin, 9–10 inches in
   diameter
½ cup milk
Salt and pepper

GARNISH
Parsley or watercress

Stir in seasonings and mix well.

Add the wine; allow the stew to cook covered for 5 minutes. Add the beef broth. Bring to a simmer on top of the stove. Cover and place in the oven at 325° or whatever temperature will maintain a simmer. Cook 1–1½ hours, or until meat is tender.

Add all of the vegetables except the corn. The carrots take the longest to cook so they should be diced small. Cook 20–30 minutes or until vegetables are tender. Add the corn 10 minutes before the stew is done.

Remove the stew from the oven.

Degrease and check seasoning.

For serving later, allow stew to cool before refrigerating. To reheat, remove hardened fat from the surface and bring slowly to a simmer on the top of the stove. Turn oven up to 350° if stew is to be served in a pumpkin.

Cut a generous top off the pumpkin, remove seeds, and scrape out the fibers, being careful not to make a hole in the bottom. Rinse the pumpkin with milk and sprinkle with salt and pepper. Place the pumpkin with its lid beside it on foil in the oven. Cook about ¾–1 hour or until the flesh of the pumpkin is tender but not too soft when pricked with a fork. (The stew will cook it a little more.) Reheat stew on the top of the stove; carefully ladle it into the pumpkin. Bring to the table with the lid on, surrounded by parsley or watercress.

Chili con Carne

cook in:

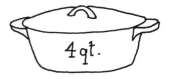

4 qt.

serve in same, or:

9" x 12"

This is a Chili made with small chunks of beef instead of the usual ground beef. The cumin and orégano give it added zest. This may be served with tortillas or Saffron Rice* or crusty bread and a big salad dressed with oil and vinegar that incorporates wedges of avocado and tomato, thinly sliced red onion, and strips of green pepper. Black olives, anchovies, and pickled peppers might be added, too. A bowl of grated sharp Cheddar cheese can be offered for sprinkling on the Chili. Seviche* would be an appetizing and unusual first course; so would melon with thinly sliced Serrano ham or Prosciutto.

Margaritas are splendid cocktails to have before Chili. Into a shaker full of ice cubes squeeze the juice of half a lime; add half an ounce of Triple Sec and two ounces of Tequila. Shake well and strain into a cocktail glass whose rim has been rubbed with the lime, then dipped in coarse salt. Mexican beer is best with Chili, but a dry white wine like Muscadet or a flowery one like Sylvaner also tastes good.

A sherbet of lemon or lime is the lightest and coolest of desserts, fresh pineapple is a little more tropical, and a rich chocolate cake is best of all.

MEAT
2 pounds beef, top or bottom round or chuck fillet, in ½–¾-inch cubes

Turn on oven to 325°.

Dry meat on paper towels. It won't brown if it is wet.

FAT
2 tablespoons cooking oil, more if needed

In a large, heavy skillet, brown the meat, a few pieces at a time, spacing them well in the pan and removing them to a lidded flameproof casserole as they are browned.

POT VEGETABLES
1 onion, chopped
1 green pepper, chopped

Cook onion and green pepper in skillet until the onion is golden and wilted. Add to the casserole.

THICKENING
1 tablespoon flour

Sprinkle flour on mixture, and stir until flour disappears.

LIQUIDS
Liquid from 3 cans kidney beans
10½-ounce can tomato purée
Hot water if needed

Add the liquid from beans. Add tomato purée.

SEASONINGS
2 cloves garlic, chopped
1 tablespoon salt
½ teaspoon cayenne pepper
1 teaspoon dried orégano
½ teaspoon ground cumin
2 tablespoons or more chili powder
1 tablespoon paprika

Mash the garlic and salt together and add to casserole with the rest of seasonings. Stir and bring to a simmer. Cover casserole and place in oven at 325° or whatever temperature will maintain a simmer. Cook 1½–2 hours, until beef is tender. Stir occasionally and add hot water in small quantities if liquid gets too thick. Check seasoning and add more chili powder if desired.

ADDED VEGETABLE
3 one-pound cans kidney beans from which liquid has been drained and used as above (more beans, if you wish)

Add beans, stir carefully, bring back to simmer on top of stove, cover and return to oven. Cook another 15–20 minutes or until beans are well heated. Check seasoning again after adding beans.

To reheat, bring casserole to room temperature if it has been refrigerated and place in preheated 325° oven for 30–45 minutes.

GARNISH
2 tablespoons chopped whole pimientos

Sprinkle pimientos over the stew.

This Chinese stew with ginger, star anise, and soy sauce is called *Pak King Ngau Yuk* (Peking Beef). It cannot be made without the star anise seed, soy sauce, and fresh ginger. (See p. 232 for sources.) It calls for slow simmering, can be made ahead of time, and is even better when it is reheated. The varieties of texture in shin beef give the dish its character, according to Jim Lee, from whose Chinese cookbook this recipe has been adapted. Plain spinach, peas, or Chinese Broccoli* makes a good accompaniment, along with boiled rice.

A white wine like Pouilly-Fumé or the Swiss Fendant, or even a rosé from Anjou or Tavel, suits this stew. The wine could also be served with a first course of boiled Cold Shrimp with Green Sauce.* The dessert should contrast with the faintly licorice taste of the star anise. A bowl of fresh fruit or a rich and crumbly tart or pastry, served with glasses of chilled Poire from Switzerland and small cups of black coffee, would be perfect.

cook in:

3 qt.

serve in same, or:

2½ qt.

Turn on oven to 325°.

FAT
2 tablespoons cooking oil,
more if needed

Heat a heavy skillet, add the oil, then the salt.

SEASONINGS
¼ teaspoon salt
2 cloves garlic, peeled and crushed
3 slices peeled fresh ginger
1 medium onion, chopped

Turn heat down to medium, add garlic, ginger, and onion. Stir-fry until just golden. The onion is listed here as a seasoning because it is more to flavor the oil than to serve as a vegetable. Remove the garlic, ginger, and onion from the skillet. Reserve for later.

MEAT
2½ pounds shin beef,
boned, in 1½–2-inch
pieces

Wipe the meat and dry it for browning. Trim off fat.

Heat the skillet again; brown the pieces of beef on all sides, a few at a time. As they are done remove them to a heavy, lidded flameproof casserole or Dutch oven.

ADDED SEASONINGS
½ teaspoon cracked black
pepper
2 star anise seeds
1 teaspoon monosodium
glutamate
2 tablespoons brown
sugar
½ teaspoon sesame oil
(optional)
2 tablespoons vinegar

Add the seasonings to the meat in the casserole.

LIQUIDS
¼ cup soy sauce
¼ cup medium-dry Sherry

Add the soy sauce and Sherry. Turn heat on under casserole, cover, and cook 2 or 3 minutes. Put in the garlic, ginger, and onions which you reserved after stir-frying.

POT VEGETABLE
3 scallions, cut in half,
including green ends

Add scallions. The sauce will be strained so don't worry about things in it.

ADDED LIQUID
Water to barely cover
Hot water if needed
during cooking

Add water to barely cover the meat. Bring to a boil, then turn down to a simmer. Cover and place in the oven at 325° or whatever temperature will just maintain a simmer. Cook 2–2½ hours or until meat is fork tender.

Remove the meat from the sauce to a clean casserole. Strain the sauce, discard solids, skim off fat.

THICKENING
2 tablespoons cornstarch mixed with ¼ cup cold water

Add the cornstarch mixture to the sauce; cook 1 or 2 minutes to thicken. Pour sauce over meat in the casserole. For later serving, allow to cool in the liquid partially covered before refrigerating. Reheat by placing in a preheated 325° oven for 30–45 minutes after removing hardened fat from the surface and bringing to room temperature.

TO FINISH

If the liquid is too thin, add more cornstarch mixed with water, 1 teaspoon at a time, until it is the thickness you want. Cook 1–2 minutes after each addition. The sauce should not completely cover the meat. If there is an excess, remove some and serve it in a bowl, or save it to warm up with any leftover stew.

GARNISH
2 scallions, green part only

Cut the green part of the scallions across in ¼-inch slices, to make little green circles. Sprinkle over the stew.

star anise
actual size

Veal

Etuvée de Veau au Vin Blanc   for 4–6   1½–2 hours to cook

cook in:

2½ qt.

serve in:

8" x 10"

Cooking *à l'étuvée* involves stewing very slowly with very little liquid, in a tightly covered pot; the ingredients practically stew in their own juices. The amount of liquid is flexible, a cup or so often being considered "a little." For variation, this stew can be made with red wine, or even a rosé. The wine is to keep the veal from sticking and makes a rich sauce. Rice is a good accompaniment but boiled new potatoes contribute a fresh garden taste.

This stew is set off well by a crisp beginning—cauliflower, celery, radishes, and carrot sticks, with a spicy Mayonnaise* for dipping. A good light red wine tastes best with veal, something like a four-year-old Volnay or a six-year-old Graves, which can be finished with a cheese course of Crema Danica or other soft cheeses. A green salad of garden lettuce might precede the cheese. French pastry might follow; for a lighter dessert, melon served with Ruby or White Port can come before the coffee and Cognac.

Turn on oven to 325°.

Dry meat on paper towels. It won't brown if it is damp.

MEAT
  3 pounds boneless veal
    shoulder in 1½-inch
    cubes

FATS
2 tablespoons butter
2 tablespoons oil

LIQUIDS
1½ cups dry white wine,
Graves Blanc Supérieur
or California Mountain
White
½ cup hot water, more if
needed

SEASONINGS
2 teaspoons salt
2 cloves garlic, chopped
¼ teaspoon thyme
2 tablespoons finely
chopped fresh parsley
¼ teaspoon pepper

THICKENING
2 tablespoons flour
¼ cup water

In a heavy skillet, heat the butter and oil. Carefully brown the pieces of veal, a few at a time, removing them as they are done to a heavy, lidded flameproof casserole. Turn heat on very low under casserole.

Add the wine; bring to a simmer; add water.

Mash together the salt and garlic on a saucer, using a strong fork. Add to the casserole with the other seasonings.

Return to a simmer, then cover and place in the oven at 325° or whatever temperature will just maintain a simmer.

Cook 1–1½ hours or until veal is almost tender. Stir occasionally during cooking. Add a little hot water if needed to keep liquid at original level. Check and correct seasoning. Skim off fat.

Mix the flour and water to a smooth paste. Stir into the casserole. Cover the casserole, put back in the oven for 15–30 minutes or until the veal is fork tender. Tip pot, skim off fat again.

For later serving, allow to cool with lid askew so the meat will not continue to cook in its own heat. Cover and refrigerate when cool.

To reheat, bring to room temperature, place in preheated 325° oven for 30–45 minutes or until stew is just bubbling and warmed through.

¾ pound sautéed mush-
rooms
¼ cup finely chopped fresh
parsley

Spread mushrooms over the stew.

Sprinkle with parsley.

Veal Paprikash

for 4–6   1½–2 hours to cook

On first reading, this recipe for a Hungarian goulash seems almost identical to the one for Boeuf à la Hongroise,* but even if both were made with the same meat they would still taste quite different. There is more garlic in the beef recipe and mashing it with the salt makes it stronger still. Here it is minced and cooked with the peppers and onions, yielding a more delicate flavor. The liquid is quite different. Here the herbs are added with the paprika, and there is less parsley. Sour cream is used to finish the Paprikash, which tastes better with fine noodles or Butter Dumplings* than with potatoes.

This Paprikash calls for a light red wine like Volnay or Santenay or a chilled dry white wine like Pouilly-Fumé or a Pinot Chardonnay from California. Crabmeat in Aspic* would be a good first course; chilled cooked green beans with oil and vinegar make a good salad. Light cheeses like Taleggio or Bel Paese taste good with the last of the wine. A tart or strudel, with chilled Poire or Kirsch and coffee, provides a pleasing finish.

cook in:

3 qt.

serve in:

2½ qt.

MEAT
3 pounds boneless veal
shoulder in 1½-inch
pieces

Turn on oven to 325°.

Dry meat on paper towels. It won't brown if it is damp.

FATS

2 tablespoons butter,
more as needed
2 tablespoons oil, more as
needed

In a large heavy skillet, heat the butter and oil.

POT VEGETABLES

4 medium onions, chopped
3 medium green peppers,
coarsely chopped
1 garlic clove, minced

Slowly cook the onions and green peppers with the garlic until they are tender but not browned. Remove with a slotted spoon to a heavy, lidded flameproof casserole. In the skillet, brown the veal on all sides, a few pieces at a time, removing them to the casserole as they are done. Use more butter and oil if necessary. Turn on heat very low under casserole.

SEASONINGS

2 tablespoons Hungarian
paprika
2 teaspoons salt
¼ teaspoon white pepper
½ teaspoon thyme
1 bay leaf
2 tablespoons finely
chopped fresh parsley

Add the paprika; stir to coat the meat evenly. Mix in the rest of the seasonings.

THICKENING

2 tablespoons flour

Sprinkle flour, a little at a time, onto the contents of the casserole. Stir with a wooden spoon until the flour disappears.

1 cup tomato purée
¼ cup tarragon vinegar, or
  ¼ teaspoon dried tarra-
  gon and ¼ cup cider
  vinegar
Canned chicken broth to
  barely cover (1–2 cups)
Hot water, if needed

Add the liquids, stirring carefully with the wooden spoon to detach any bits stuck on the bottom of the pot.

Bring to a simmer, cover and place in the preheated oven at 325°. Turn down to 300° or whatever temperature will just maintain a simmer. Cook 1½–2 hours or until veal is fork tender. Check during cooking, stir, and add hot water if necessary to keep stew from sticking.

Tip pot and skim off fat. Check and correct seasoning. Remove to a clean casserole if the cooking vessel is messy.

For later serving, allow to cool with lid askew (so it won't further cook in its own heat), cover, and refrigerate. To reheat bring to room temperature; place in preheated 325° oven for 30–45 minutes or until stew is just bubbling and warmed through.

TO FINISH
½ cup sour cream

Remove ½ cup liquid from stew. Gradually stir it into the sour cream. Stir into the stew. Use more sour cream if desired. Bring gently back to a simmer, but do not boil.

GARNISHES
2 pimientos, coarsely
  chopped
¼ cup finely chopped fresh
  parsley

Strew the pimientos on top; sprinkle with parsley.

Stufatino

for 4   1½–2 hours to cook

This Stufatino is a Florentine specialty. It is made with slices of leg of veal less than half an inch thick cooked in white wine with rosemary.

cook in:

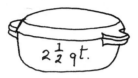

$2\frac{1}{2}$ qt.

serve in same or:

8" X 10"

MEAT
2 pounds leg of veal in ⅜-inch slices

FAT
1 tablespoon butter
1 tablespoon olive oil, more if needed
2 slices bacon, diced

POT VEGETABLE
1 onion, sliced

SEASONINGS
2 cloves garlic, chopped
1½ teaspoons salt
3 or 4 grinds of the peppermill
¼ teaspoon rosemary
2 tablespoons tomato paste

Roman versions often call for beef and red wine, and the rosemary is replaced by orégano or marjoram. If the meat is cooked in a chunk, it is called *stufato*. Try the Stufatino with parsleyed potatoes or a Risotto.*

The perfect wine for the stew is Chianti, to go also with an antipasto before and the Fontina or Taleggio cheese that comes after. An alternative first course might be fettuccine with garlic and butter sauce. A salad of garden lettuce can follow the Stufatino. Fresh fruit is the sensible dessert, but an extravaganza like cold poached pears with hot Zabaglione might be more exciting, with Strega and espresso.

Turn oven to 325°.

Trim fat from meat. Dry slices for browning. They won't brown if they are damp.

In a skillet, heat the butter and oil, and slowly cook the bacon until it is lightly brown. Remove the bacon with a slotted spoon to a heavy, lidded flameproof casserole.

In the skillet, cook the onion until it is limp and golden, then remove it to the casserole. In the same skillet brown the veal slices on both sides, and remove them to the casserole, turning on a very low flame under it.

In a saucer mash the garlic with the salt, using a strong fork. Add to casserole with the other seasonings.

    1 cup dry white wine,
       Orvieto or Soave
    Hot water to barely cover
       (about 1 cup, more if
       needed)

Add wine. Simmer stew on the top of the stove until wine is reduced to half. Add enough hot water to barely cover the meat. Bring back to a simmer.

Cover casserole and place in the oven at 325°, or whatever temperature is needed to just maintain the simmer. Cook 1½–2 hours, or until meat is fork tender. Check occasionally during the cooking to make sure the liquid has not boiled away. Add a little hot water if stew looks too dry. When the meat is done, tip the pot and skim fat. Check the seasoning.

For serving at this time, arrange the slices of veal in a clean warm casserole (the one used for cooking will look rather messy) or a warm oval baking dish, and pour the sauce over them. For later serving, allow to cool; cover the casserole with its lid or the baking dish with foil. To reheat, allow casserole to come to room temperature. Then place it in a preheated 325° oven for 30–45 minutes.

Sprinkle with parsley.

GARNISH
    ¼ cup finely chopped fresh
       parsley

Ternera al Jerez

for 6   about 1½ hours to cook

The Sherry and the cumin give this Spanish veal stew a deliciously different taste. Traditionally, it is served with potatoes home-fried in olive oil and a salad of red and green sweet peppers and ripe olives, but Saffron Rice* and a lettuce salad are also good with it. The pimientos and olives can be added to the stew at the end, as garnish.

cook in:

2½ qt.

serve in:

8" x 10"

MEAT
3 pounds boneless veal
shoulder, in 1½-inch
cubes

MARINADE
¾ cup Fino Sherry
¾ cup water
1 tablespoon olive oil

FATS
1 tablespoon butter
1 tablespoon olive oil
2 slices bacon, diced

POT VEGETABLE
2 medium onions, sliced

A red wine of Rioja, or even a white Alella, would be better than the coarser Valdepeñas. Better still would be the fuller and rounder wines of the Rhône—a Châteauneuf-du-Pape or Côte Rôtie five or six years old or a Tavel rosé, or a younger and fresher white Hermitage. A first course of chorizos, Spanish sausages, sliced and fried, would be delicious with very cold Manzanilla Sherry, the driest wine in the world. A Spanish melon or flan is a traditional dessert, served with a cream Sherry, although a Ruby Port is even better with melon, followed by black coffee laced with dry Spanish anisette, either Chinchon or Ojen Secco.

Turn on oven to 325°.

Trim fat from veal and wipe with damp paper towels.

Place veal in a nonmetallic bowl and pour marinade over it. Let it stand 2–3 hours, stirring occasionally. Drain, discarding the marinade. Diluted wine seems to draw off a lot of blood and the marinade is too cloudy to cook the stew in. Dry the meat well on paper towels. It will not brown if it is wet.

In a skillet, heat the butter and oil. Slowly cook the bacon until it renders its fat and is golden but not too brown. With a slotted spoon, remove it to a heavy, lidded flameproof casserole.

In the skillet slowly cook the onions until they are limp and golden, not brown, and remove them to the casserole. Use more oil if necessary.

Brown the veal in the same skillet, a few pieces at a time, removing them to the casserole as they are done. Turn heat on very low under the casserole.

THICKENING
  2 tablespoons flour

SEASONINGS
  2 garlic cloves, chopped
  2 teaspoons salt
  1 teaspoon cumin
  3 or 4 grinds of the
    peppermill

LIQUIDS
  1 cup Fino Sherry,
    brought to a boil
  ½ cup boiling water
  Hot water, if needed

GARNISHES
  2 whole pimientos, in
    strips
  10–12 black olives
  ¼ cup finely chopped fresh
    parsley

Sprinkle flour on the meat and onions in the casserole, stirring gently until the flour disappears.

On a saucer, mash the garlic with the salt, using a strong fork. Add to the casserole with the other seasonings.

Pour in the hot Sherry, stir carefully to detach any bits stuck on the bottom, and add water. Bring to a simmer.

Cover and place in the oven at 325°. Turn down to 300° or whatever temperature will just maintain the simmer.

Cook 1½ hours or until the veal is tender. Check occasionally during cooking. If liquid has cooked down too much, add hot water in ½-cup amounts, as needed. For later serving, allow stew to cool with lid askew so it will not cook further. When cool, cover, and refrigerate. To reheat, bring to room temperature, place in a preheated 325° oven for 30–45 minutes or until stew is bubbling and warmed through.

Sprinkle with pimientos, black olives, and parsley.

Lamb

Navarin Printanier

for 6   1½–1¾ hours to cook

cook in:

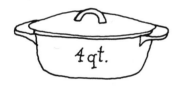

4 qt.

serve in:

9" x 12"

Lamb stew with spring vegetables is served in Paris whenever small white onions and new potatoes are in the market, but it really doesn't taste like spring until the chestnuts blossom and there are new peas, baby carrots, and white turnips to add too. This is perhaps the best known of the brown ragoûts, and when the meat is not browned and water is used for the cooking liquid, the dish is dubbed à l'Anglaise and is very much like Irish stew. The method here calls for shoulder, with stock and white wine as liquid. Tradition calls for lamb chuck, with a little sugar for browning, and water as the liquid. Every cook develops personal variations.

April is the last oyster month, and oysters on the half shell are often served as a first course with a bottle of Chablis or white Graves, but Consommé* seems to suit the taste as well. Early asparagus may replace both when it becomes available. Burgundians say a Côte de Beaune is best with Navarin, but most Parisians prefer a good château-bottled Bordeaux, maybe ten years old, to be finished with a cheese course, after a salad of garden lettuce. The perfect dessert is *fraises de bois,* wild strawberries, with cream, followed by Chartreuse Verte and coffee, but these rarely arrive until May, when taste turns to racks and barons and legs of lamb. It is a glorious spring in Paris when the hankering for Navarin coincides with chestnut blossoms, new asparagus, the last of the oysters, and the first of the wild strawberries.

Turn on oven to 325°.

Trim fat from lamb and dry the pieces on paper towels. They won't brown if they are damp.

In a skillet, heat the butter and oil, and carefully brown the lamb, a few pieces at a time. As they are done remove them to a heavy, lidded 3–4-quart flameproof casserole. Turn a medium heat on under the casserole.

Sprinkle sugar on the meat; stir and cook until sugar browns. Turn heat down to low under the casserole.

Sprinkle flour on the lamb, a little at a time, turning and stirring to spread it through the meat. Stir until the flour is browned and disappears.

Add the seasonings.

MEAT
   3 pounds boneless lamb shoulder in 1½-inch pieces

FATS
   2 tablespoons butter
   2 tablespoons oil

COLORING
   2 teaspoons sugar

THICKENING
   2 tablespoons flour

SEASONINGS
   1 teaspoon salt
   ¼ teaspoon white pepper
   2 garlic cloves, minced
   ¼ teaspoon rosemary
   ¼ teaspoon thyme
   1 bay leaf
   2 tablespoons finely chopped fresh parsley

POT VEGETABLE
   3 ripe tomatoes, peeled,
      seeded, and chopped, or
      1 one-pound can,
      drained and chopped

Add the tomatoes.

LIQUIDS
   ½ cup dry white wine,
      Graves Blanc or
      Chablis
   2 cups canned beef broth,
      or enough to barely
      cover

Add the liquid, stirring to incorporate the flour and season-ings, and to dislodge bits stuck to the bottom of the casse-role. Bring to a simmer.

Cover the casserole and place in the oven at 325°. Turn down to 300° or whatever temperature will just maintain a sim-mer. Cook 1 hour.

ADDED VEGETABLES
   12 small new potatoes, in
      skins, or 6 medium pota-
      toes, peeled and halved
   6 medium carrots in
      2-inch pieces
   6 white turnips, halved
   12–18 small white onions

Wash and peel the vegetables. If little new potatoes are used, scrub but do not peel. Split the thick-end pieces of carrot to make them equal in size to the small-end ones. Make a small cross in the root ends of the onions. They will cook more evenly and will be less likely to separate. Put the vegetables carefully into the stew. Cover and cook ½–¾ hour longer, until meat and vegetables are tender. Tip pot; skim off fat. Check seasoning.

For later serving, allow stew to cool with lid askew so it won't continue to cook in its own heat. To reheat, bring to room temperature if stew has been refrigerated; place in a preheated 325° oven for 30 minutes, or until stew is just bubbling and warmed through.

TO FINISH
   ½ pound fresh green beans
      in 2-inch pieces
   ½ cup boiling water
   ¼ teaspoon salt
   1 tablespoon butter

Cook beans in water, salt, and butter in a covered saucepan for about 10–12 minutes, until tender but still crisp. Add to stew. The green beans are added at the end so that they are still bright green and serve as a garnish.

Blanquette d'Agneau à l'Ancienne

cook in:

serve in:

9" x 12"

Whoever heard of a browned blanquette? It should be white, as the name suggests, but rambling around Paris twenty years ago, James Beard and Alexander Watt found this recipe for their *Paris Cuisine* at La Calvados. There the lamb was browned, and the dish ended up a golden, creamy lamb stew with Madeira, tiny white onions, and mushrooms, served with croutons. Applied to a blanquette, *à l'Ancienne,* "the old lady's way," is just a fancy name for a classic dish of *la cuisine bourgeoise,* but it also means using a velouté and Madeira. This impeccable dish can be served with new potatoes, noodles, or plain rice.

A fine old château bottling of Bordeaux, a claret at least ten years old, brings out the elegance of the Blanquette. A first course of smoked salmon with capers and a bottle of Champagne, or a soft white Graves, might go before. A lettuce and watercress salad could precede a cheese course of splendid Brie or Boursault. Dessert should be a miracle of the pâtisserie, perhaps a dacquoise or a croquembouche, with Champagne.

VELOUTÉ

2 tablespoons butter
2 tablespoons flour
2 cups canned chicken broth
½ cup heavy cream, more if needed

This sauce goes into the stew later, but it is a good idea to make it first. In a saucepan, melt the butter and blend in the flour. Add the chicken broth; stir and cook until it thickens. Add the cream. Put aside.

MEAT

3 pounds boneless lamb shoulder, in 1½-inch pieces

Dry the meat on paper towels. It won't brown if it is damp.

FATS
2 tablespoons butter
2 tablespoons oil, more if
needed

In a large (11- or 12-inch) enamelware or stainless-steel skillet, heat the fat and brown the lamb well on all sides, a few pieces at a time. As they are done remove them to a heavy, lidded flameproof casserole. Turn the heat on low under the casserole and cook the meat uncovered 15–20 minutes, shaking the casserole occasionally to prevent sticking.

SEASONINGS
1 teaspoon salt
½ teaspoon white pepper

Stir the salt and pepper into the casserole.

While the meat is cooking in the casserole, pour the leftover fat out of the skillet.

LIQUIDS
½ cup Madeira
The velouté (see above)

Pour the Madeira into the skillet; stir to dislodge any stuck particles. Add the velouté to the Madeira in the skillet; allow to boil briskly for 5 minutes. Strain and add to the meat in the casserole, stirring well with a wooden spoon to incorporate any brown on the bottom of the casserole. Bring to a simmer, then place in oven at 325°. Turn down to 300° or whatever temperature will just maintain the simmer. Cook ½–¾ hour or until meat is beginning to be tender.

ADDED VEGETABLES
12–18 small white onions
1 pound small button
mushrooms

Peel the onions; cut a small cross in the root end to help prevent them from separating. Trim the stems of the mushrooms and wipe them clean with damp paper towels. If you use large mushrooms, cut them in ¼-inch slices.

ADDITIONAL FAT
½ pound butter, clarified
(see p. 235 for clarifying
butter in quantity)

To clarify butter, heat it in a small saucepan until it foams but does not brown. Skim off the foam, and pour the clear butter off the white sediment in the bottom. It is the milky solids which make butter burn quickly.

In a clean skillet, sauté the onions and mushrooms in 3 tablespoons of the clarified butter until they are lightly browned. Add to the casserole.

Cook ½ to ¾ hour more or until meat and vegetables are tender. If the liquid has cooked down too much, add more heavy cream and allow the stew to heat up again. Check seasoning.

For immediate serving turn into a clean, warm casserole or baking dish.

For later serving, allow stew to cool, and cover with lid or foil. To reheat, allow dish to come to room temperature and place in preheated 325° oven for 30–45 minutes.

TO FINISH
6 slices bread with crusts removed
6 thin slices lemon
¼ cup finely chopped fresh parsley

Fry the bread in the rest of the clarified butter, starting with 2 tablespoons and adding more whenever the pan dries. Cut each slice into 4 triangles. Arrange around the edge of the stew, lay the lemon slices in a row down the middle, and sprinkle parsley over all.

The bread can be done ahead and reheated for 5 minutes in the oven spread out on a piece of foil.

Abbacchio alla Ciociara

for 6   1–1½ hours to cook

cook in:
2½ qt.

serve in:
8" x 10"

When spring comes to Rome, baby lamb comes to the market. Romeo Salta's version, using our lamb, incorporating ham and braising in Cognac, comes from the Lazio town of Ciociara. Green beans are included here because they go so well with rosemary. While a thin pasta like fettuccine is excellent, matchstick potatoes or home fries would be just as good. This dish is really a braise, which cooks in very little liquid; the method is simple but demands attention.

Abbacchio calls for a good red Chianti or Bardolino, a first course of Consommé* or asparagus, hot or cold, and diced green pepper in a salad of garden lettuce. A range of soft Italian cheeses—Fontina, Taleggio—might precede a dessert with strawberries, served with Asti Spumante.

MEATS
3 pounds shoulder of lamb in 1-inch cubes
¼ pound prosciutto or cooked ham, cut in ¼-inch julienne strips

FATS
2 tablespoons butter
2 tablespoons oil, more if needed

SEASONINGS
2 cloves garlic, minced
½ teaspoon rosemary
2 teaspoons salt
½ teaspoon freshly ground black pepper

LIQUIDS
½ cup Cognac
Boiling water as needed during cooking

TO FINISH
½ pound fresh green beans, whole
½ cup boiling water
¼ teaspoon salt
1 tablespoon butter

Turn on oven to 325°.

Dry lamb on paper towels. It won't brown if it is damp.

In a skillet, brown the lamb carefully in the hot fat, a few pieces at a time, removing them to a heavy, lidded flame-proof casserole as they are done. Turn on heat very low under the casserole. Add the ham to the lamb and cook 5 minutes uncovered.

Stir in the garlic, allowing it to cook 1 or 2 minutes but not to brown.

Stir in the rest of the seasonings.

Add the Cognac. Bring to a simmer. Cover; place in the oven. Turn down to 300° or whatever temperature will just maintain a simmer. Cook 1–1½ hours or until lamb is tender, checking frequently. If the liquid cooks away, add boiling water in ½-cup amounts as needed during cooking.

Cook the green beans in a covered saucepan with the water, salt and butter for 10–12 minutes. They should be tender, but still crisp and bright green. Stir drained beans into stew. Omit beans if stew is to be reheated.

For immediate serving, turn the stew into a clean warm casserole or baking dish. For later serving, allow to cool, cover the casserole with its lid or the baking dish with foil.

To reheat bring the dish to room temperature and place in a preheated 325° oven for 30–45 minutes. Add beans and, if you wish, sprinkle with chopped parsley.

Abbacchio alla Romano

cook in:

2½ qt.

serve in:

8" x 10"

The Romans dote on suckling lamb, *abbacchio,* which is usually spitted or roasted. Occasionally, they cut up the meat into a casserole, adding peppers and a few anchovies. As lambs get older, the Romans add more anchovies, herbs, and garlic. The Italian cook is a master of this balancing act, using materials from the garden as often as possible. This recipe is suited to our lamb, and green beans are used rather than the more customary peppers at the end, just because beans are so good with rosemary. If peppers are preferred, try the recipe with dry Vermouth instead of the white wine. Rice or pasta is a good accompaniment, and so is a Risotto* with saffron and cheese.

A white Soave or Frascati is good with both the stew and a first course of salami, olives, and celery; if a risotto is served, a red wine like a Chianti or Nebbiolo would be better.

A salad of rugula (rocket, in English) or spring greens is best, followed by some typically Italian dessert like Zabaglione or pastries with custard fillings.

Turn oven on to 325°.

Dry meat on paper towels. It won't brown if it is damp.

MEAT
2 pounds boned shoulder of lamb, in 1½-inch pieces

FAT
¼ cup olive oil

In a skillet, heat the oil and brown the lamb thoroughly, a few pieces at a time. As they are done remove them to a lidded flameproof casserole.

SEASONINGS

1 clove garlic, minced
½ teaspoon salt
3 or 4 grinds of the
    peppermill
½ teaspoon rosemary
½ teaspoon sage

Stir in the garlic. Add the rest of the seasonings to the meat in the casserole, mixing well.

THICKENING

1 tablespoon flour

Sprinkle the flour over the stew, stirring until flour disappears.

LIQUIDS

½ cup white wine (Graves
    Blanc or Mountain
    White)
½ cup wine vinegar
½ cup water
Hot water in ½-cup
    amounts, as needed

Add the liquids and stir. Bring to a simmer on top of the stove.

Cover pot and place in oven at 300° or whatever temperature will maintain a simmer.

Cook 45 minutes to 1 hour. If the lamb is not fork tender, cook longer. Check occasionally for dryness. If the liquid has cooked away, add hot water in ½-cup amounts, stirring carefully to clear the bottom of the casserole.

TO FINISH

½ pound fresh green
    beans in 2-inch pieces
½ cup boiling water
¼ teaspoon salt
1 tablespoon butter
3 anchovy fillets, chopped

Cook green beans in a covered saucepan with the water, salt, and butter for 10–12 minutes. They should be tender but still crisp and bright green. If stew is to be served later, cook beans at time of reheating.

Stir the anchovies into the stew. Degrease the stew and check seasoning. Since the anchovies are salty, this recipe calls for a minimum of salt; you may now want to add more.

Turn into a clean hot casserole or baking dish that will accommodate the added beans. Mix in drained beans or arrange them at either end of the dish with some sauce spooned over them.

For later serving, omit beans, cover, and refrigerate. Add freshly cooked and drained beans to reheated stew. To reheat, place the covered casserole or well-covered baking dish in a preheated 325° oven for 30–45 minutes, or until stew is bubbling and warmed through. If the dish has been in the refrigerator, bring to room temperature before placing in the oven.

GARNISH
¼ cup finely chopped fresh parsley

Sprinkle parsley over the stew.

Lamb Pilaf

for 4   ¾–1 hour

cook in:

2½ qt.

serve in same, or

8" x 10"

Pilaf, or Pilaw, or Pilau, is an Oriental rice dish containing all sorts of good things, from pine kernels to chick peas. Here, it contains prunes and raisins with a dice of lamb, and doesn't end up tasting as sweet as one would imagine.

It is delicious with a flowery wine like a Riesling or a soft Italian Soave.

Chorizos, Spanish sausages, are a good first course when they are sliced and quickly sautéed for serving with drinks or some of the wine. Garden lettuce and thinly sliced cucumbers make a cooling salad. Lime sherbet adds a further fresh flavor for dessert. A hostess with help or a cook with an excess of time and energy might wish to make a soufflé, which would naturally call for a bottle of Champagne. Soufflé is hard to manage with a stew, so just the Champagne would do, served with Champagne biscuits, or gaufrettes. A sliver of sponge cake mounded with whipped cream is remarkably good with Champagne, too. Macaroons or gingersnaps can be crumbled over the whipped cream.

FRUITS
    8–10 prunes, pitted
    ⅓ cup seedless yellow
       raisins
    Boiling water

Cut each prune into 4 pieces; place with the raisins in a small bowl. Cover with boiling water and allow to stand for ½–1 hour.

MEAT
    1½ pounds boneless lamb
       shoulder in ¾-inch cubes

Trim fat from the lamb. Dry the pieces on a paper towel. They won't brown if they are damp.

FATS
    1 slice bacon, diced
    1 tablespoon butter
    1 tablespoon oil, more if
       needed

In a 2½- or 3-quart lidded flameproof casserole, slowly cook the bacon in the butter and oil, until it is golden. Push to the side of the casserole.

Add the pieces of lamb, a few at a time, pushing them to the side as they brown. Use more oil if needed, but remove any left in casserole after browning the meat.

POT VEGETABLE
    2 medium onions, chopped

Add the onions. Stir and cook gently until they are limp.

SEASONINGS
    1 teaspoon salt
    ¼ teaspoon black pepper

Sprinkle with salt and pepper.

LIQUID
    1 cup canned beef broth

Add broth, cover, and simmer on low flame for 25 minutes. Turn on oven to 325°.

ADDITIONAL SEASONINGS
    ⅛ teaspoon crushed red
       pepper
    1 teaspoon turmeric
    1 small bay leaf
    1 teaspoon curry powder
    6 thin lemon slices

Add the rest of the seasonings. More red pepper can be added if desired. Cayenne pepper or Tabasco can be used instead. Add the drained prunes and raisins.

ADDITIONAL LIQUID
   1½ cups canned beef
      broth, more if needed

Add the broth; bring to a simmer.

RICE
   ¾ cup uncooked rice

Add the rice, bring to a simmer again, cover, and place in the oven at 325° or whatever temperature will maintain a simmer.

Cook 45 minutes, or until lamb is tender and rice has swollen and absorbed liquid. Check during cooking, and if stew gets too dry, add small amounts of broth. The dish is supposed to end up moist, but not wet.

Like most rice dishes, pilaf is best served at the time it is made, but it can be reheated. For later serving, cool and refrigerate.

To reheat, bring to room temperature, stir gently, and pour in ¼ cup more broth. Cover and place in preheated 325° oven for 30–45 minutes or until pilaf is warmed through.

GARNISHES
   6 thin slices lemon
   ¼ cup finely chopped fresh
      parsley

Remove cooked lemon slices, place fresh ones on the pilaf, and sprinkle parsley over all.

CONDIMENTS
   Chutney
   Toasted slivered almonds

In little side dishes, serve chutney and almonds which have been lightly browned in butter and drained. Condiments can be as many and varied as curry condiments: pickles, chopped orange or lemon rind, crumbled bacon, guava jelly, pickled watermelon rind, etc.

Lamb and Bean Khoreshe

cook in:

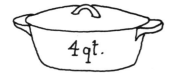

4 qt.

serve in same, or:

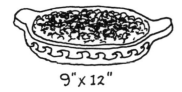

9" x 12"

A Khoreshe is a Persian stew. It has lots of vegetables to make the meat go a long way and is flavored with sour fruit juices and spices. The most famous is Qormeh Sabzi (often spelled with a G instead of a Q), nicknamed the Master of Minces. Our version calls for large cubes of lamb, but it can also be made with chicken or duck. This recipe produces a surprisingly refreshing and light-tasting stew with a hint of lemon. It is delicious served with Saffron Rice* sprinkled with slivered almonds and pistachios.

This stew is reminiscent of the eastern Mediterranean, and the pitch-flavored wine of Greece, Retsina, might be served with it. But Retsina is an acquired taste, so a California Hungarian Riesling or Italian Verdicchio is suggested. Beer is good, too. Hummus,* a paste made of chick peas and served with unleavened bread, or crackers with sesame seeds, is good with drinks, and an Italian antipasto would also be appropriate. A salad with cucumbers and oranges provides a pleasing contrast to the khoreshe, and can be followed with a dessert of fresh pears served with Feta or cream cheese. Persimmons and pomegranates would add a typical Iranian touch.

Turn on oven to 325°.

Melt the butter in a heavy, lidded flameproof casserole (or Dutch oven).

Add the vegetables and cook gently until they are limp. Turn off heat.

FAT
    4 tablespoons butter

POT VEGETABLES
    2 cups chopped fresh
      parsley
    2 bunches scallions,
      chopped
    2 cups chopped spinach

MEAT
    3 pounds boneless lamb
      shoulder in 1½-inch
      cubes

Wipe the meat and dry on paper towels. It won't brown if it is damp.

ADDITIONAL FATS
    2 tablespoons butter
    2 tablespoons oil, more if
      needed

In a heavy skillet, heat the butter and oil, then brown the lamb, a few pieces at a time. As they are done, remove them to the casserole with the vegetables.

SEASONINGS
    2 teaspoons salt
    1 teaspoon black pepper
    1 teaspoon turmeric
      (optional)
    Juice of 2 lemons
    1 lemon in 4 slices

Sprinkle with salt, stir in pepper (and turmeric if used), and add lemon juice. Place lemon slices on top.

LIQUID
    Water to barely cover

Add the liquid, bring to a simmer, cover, and place in the oven at 325° or whatever temperature will just maintain a simmer. Cook 1–1½ hours or until lamb is fork tender. Remove lemon slices and discard. Tip pot, skim off fat.

ADDED VEGETABLE
    3 one-pound cans white
      beans (without sauce),
      drained, or cooked dried
      beans (see Note)

Drain beans, reserving liquid. Carefully stir beans into stew. Adjust seasoning. Cover and cook until beans are hot. Add bean liquid if stew is too dry.

For later serving, cool with lid askew, so the stew won't continue to cook in its own heat. When cool, cover and refrigerate. To reheat, bring to room temperature, place in preheated 325° oven for 30–45 minutes, or until stew is just bubbling and heated through.

GARNISH
    1 lemon thinly sliced

Arrange lemon slices on top.

Note: To use dried beans: Wash and pick over 2 cups (1 pound) dried white beans, or dried Great Northern, navy, or baby lima beans. Cover with water, bring to a boil, boil 2 minutes. Remove from heat, cover and allow to soak for 1 hour. Drain beans, place in 6 cups of water, add 2 teaspoons salt, and bring to a boil. Simmer partially covered for 1½–2 hours, until beans are tender but not mushy. Drain and add to the stew as indicated.

Arni Prassa

for 4   1¼–1½ hours to cook

cook in:

3–4 qt.

serve in same

A refreshing taste of lemon and dill distinguishes this Grecian lamb stew, developed by Leon Lianides of the Coach House, in New York's Greenwich Village, one of the most distinguished restaurants in the country. The thickening with whole egg and lemon at the end makes it foamy and unlike any other stew. It is classic, light and delicious, and is meant to be served simply with crusty bread. Note that the stew is browned in the oven instead of in a skillet, a restaurant method that works well if you can get your own oven hot enough. It can, of course, be browned in the usual way.

A Beaujolais from the township of Juliénas or Brouilly or Chiroubles is excellent with this and so is the white Burgundy used in the stew, a Chablis or a Pouilly-Fuissé. Olives, anchovies on pimiento slices, and a bowl of toasted almonds, served with Raki or one of the anise-flavored liqueurs like Pec or Pernod, all of which turn cloudy when mixed with water and ice, make a fine preface to the stew. A green salad, followed by Feta cheese and more of the wine, rounds out the meal. Because the stew is light, the dessert might be rich, perhaps cake or pastry filled with custard, followed by Cognac and coffee.

MEAT
  3½ pounds boneless lamb
    shoulder in 3-inch pieces

FATS
  1 teaspoon cooking oil for
    browning the meat
  1–2 tablespoons butter, if
    needed for onions

POT VEGETABLE
  2 medium onions, finely
    chopped

SEASONINGS
  2 teaspoons salt
  1 teaspoon pepper
  1 teaspoon finely chopped
    fresh dill
  1 tablespoon finely
    chopped fresh parsley

LIQUIDS
  1 cup water
  1 cup dry white wine, a
    white Burgundy like
    Pinot Chardonnay
  ½ cup canned chicken
    broth

Turn on oven to 550°, or highest point.

Trim fat from meat, and dry it on paper towels; it won't brown if it is damp.

Oil a shallow roasting pan; place it in the preheated oven for 5 minutes to get it hot. Spread the pieces of lamb in the hot pan, not too close together or they will steam rather than brown. Do it in batches if necessary. Place in the oven for about 15–20 minutes, or until the meat is lightly browned. Shake the pan or turn the pieces once or twice to brown on all sides.

When the meat is brown, put it into a lidded flameproof 4-quart casserole. Add the onions and cook slowly on a medium flame until the meat browns a little more and the onions are tender but not brown. Add a little butter if necessary.

Mix in the seasonings.

Add the liquids, bring to a simmer, cover, and place in the oven at 325°. Turn down to 300° or whatever temperature will just maintain a simmer.

Cook 50–60 minutes or until almost tender. Tip pot and skim off fat.

ADDED VEGETABLE
6–8 medium leeks

Trim the leeks, removing the roots and most of the green. Cut in 2-inch pieces, and allow them to stand in lukewarm salted water for a few minutes. Wash very thoroughly under running water, gently spreading the leaves to remove the sand. Place them carefully on the stew. Spoon some of the liquid over them. Cover and return to the oven. Cook 20–30 minutes more, or until the leeks are tender but not overdone. Spoon liquid over the stew as it cooks, but do not stir—the leeks should not be disturbed. If liquid cooks down, add a little hot water, but only if there is danger of sticking.

For later serving, cool with lid askew, cover, and refrigerate. To reheat, bring to room temperature, place, partially covered (to avoid steaming the leeks), in a preheated 325° oven for about 30 minutes, or until stew is warmed through.

TO FINISH
1 teaspoon cornstarch
Juice of 2 lemons
4 eggs
1 cup stew liquid

With the stew out of the oven and off the heat, mix the cornstarch with the lemon juice. Beat the eggs vigorously for about 4 minutes. Gradually add the cornstarch and lemon mixture, beating constantly for another 2 minutes. Slowly stir 1 cup of hot liquid from the stew into the egg mixture, still beating, until the liquid is all in, about 2 more minutes. Pour the egg mixture over the stew, shaking casserole to mix through. Do not stir. Serve immediately.

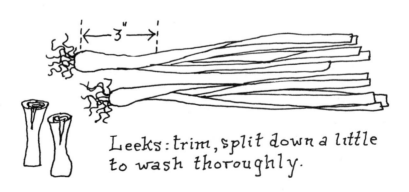

Leeks: trim, split down a little to wash thoroughly.

Pork

Brussels Pork Stew

for 6   1¼–1½ hours to cook

cook in:

4 qt.

serve in same

Brussels sprouts are easy to hate. They have a rank taste when overcooked, which they usually are. This stew may overcome prejudice, but there are those who might want to substitute endive, celery, or artichoke hearts.

A light red wine like a Beaujolais is delicious with this stew, but so is a white wine like Pouilly-Fumé or a Riesling from the Rheinhessen or the Pfalz. Hot Chicken Consommé* or dried beef with watercress would make a good first course. The salad can be endive with a julienne of beets, followed by Edam or Gouda and Brie or Camembert. An excellent dessert would be cubed pears which have been allowed to stand in lemon juice, Triple Sec, and sugar for an hour—one teaspoonful of each per cup of pear, with a dollop of sour cream stirred in and a grating of orange rind on top. Gingerbread, along with Ruby or Tawny Port, makes a delicious accompaniment.

MEAT
3 pounds boneless pork shoulder in 1½-inch cubes

Turn on oven to 325°.

(Pork loin can be used instead. Have it boned; the bones cut into serving portions, and the meat into 1½-inch cubes. About 4 pounds loin of pork would be the equivalent. Bones can be left out, but they do add flavor.)

Trim the most obvious fat from pork, and dry the pieces for browning. They won't brown if they are damp.

FAT
1 tablespoon oil, more if needed

In a skillet, heat the oil and brown the pork, a few pieces at a time. Even after trimming there will probably be enough fat rendered to brown all the meat, but if there isn't add more oil. As they are done, remove the pieces to a heavy, lidded flameproof casserole.

SEASONINGS
2 teaspoons salt
½ teaspoon freshly ground black pepper
1 teaspoon ground rosemary

If the rosemary is in the form of little sticks, grind with a mortar and pestle to make a powder. Stir the seasonings into the casserole.

Turn heat on very low under the casserole.

THICKENING
3 tablespoons flour

Stir in the flour, a little at a time, until it disappears.

LIQUIDS
1 pint beer
1½ cups canned beef broth

Add the liquids, stirring to mix everything and to dislodge any bits stuck to the bottom of the pot.

COLORING (optional)
1–2 teaspoons meat coloring, as unflavored as possible

If the stew looks too pale, add coloring.

Bring to a simmer, cover, and place in the preheated oven. Turn down to 300° or whatever temperature will just maintain the simmer. Cook 45 minutes. Tip pot and skim off fat.

ADDED VEGETABLES
  4 medium carrots in ¼-
    inch slices
  4 medium potatoes in ½-
    inch slices
  4 medium onions,
    quartered

Add the vegetables, cover the casserole, and return to the oven for 30–45 minutes or until pork and vegetables are tender. Check and correct seasoning.

For later serving, cool with lid askew so the stew will not continue to cook. When thoroughly cool, refrigerate. To reheat, bring to room temperature, place in a preheated 325° oven for 30–45 minutes or until stew is just bubbling and warmed through.

TO FINISH
  1 pound fresh Brussels
    sprouts
    or
  2 packages frozen
    Brussels sprouts

If fresh sprouts are used, peel off any bad outer leaves, trim stems, wash thoroughly, and make a small cut in the stem for more even cooking. Place in a saucepan with 1 cup boiling water and ¼ teaspoon salt. Cover and cook 5–10 minutes or until sprouts are just tender. Cook frozen sprouts according to directions on package. In either case, do not overcook. Add the sprouts to the stew. They are all the garnish you need.

Szekely Gulyàs

for 6–8   about 2–2½ hours to cook

cook in:

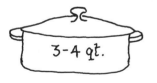

3-4 qt.

serve in same

Sauerkraut reaches noble heights in this Transylvanian pork goulash, Polish versions of which are called *bigos*. Paprika links it to Hungary, and Vienna makes a specialty of it, serving it with boiled potatoes or noodles. As in Choucroute Garnie, that glory of Alsace and of the Brasserie Lipp, the sauerkraut gains flavor from simmering in white wine with juniper berries, peppercorns, and caraway seeds.

The white wines of Austria, like Gumpoldskirchener or those of Krems, go well with this dish, but so does a red wine like Beaujolais or beer. Consommé,* hot or cold, would be a properly light first course; lettuce with sliced cucumbers and green peppers would be an equally light salad. A cheese course may be too much; dessert might be just a bowl of fruit.

Turn on oven to 325°.

FAT
    4 slices bacon, diced

In a 4-quart lidded flameproof casserole, slowly cook the bacon until it has rendered its fat and is golden brown.

POT VEGETABLES
    2 medium onions, chopped
    2 cloves garlic, minced
    2 pounds sauerkraut

Add the onions and garlic; cook slowly until they are just limp, not brown. Drain sauerkraut, squeezing out liquid by hand. Mix thoroughly with onions, garlic, and bacon. Cook 5 minutes, stirring.

SEASONINGS
    1 teaspoon caraway seeds
    12 whole peppercorns, bruised
    6 juniper berries (optional)

Stir in the seasonings. If juniper berries are not available, add 2 tablespoons gin at the end, just before adding sour cream.

LIQUIDS
    2 cups dry white wine, California Riesling or Johannisberg Riesling
    Canned chicken broth to barely cover (1–2 cups, more if needed)

Pour in the wine, add chicken broth to barely cover. Put lid on casserole, place in 325° oven. Cook 1 hour. Check occasionally, adding more broth if sauerkraut gets too dry.

MEAT
    3 pounds boneless pork shoulder in 1½–2-inch pieces

Dry the meat. It won't brown if it is damp.

ADDITIONAL FAT
2 tablespoons oil

In a skillet, heat the oil. Brown the pork on all sides, a few pieces at a time. As they are done, put them on paper towels to drain.

ADDED SEASONINGS
1 teaspoon salt
2 tablespoons Hungarian paprika

Pour fat from skillet, return meat, sprinkle with salt and paprika. Mix well.

ADDED VEGETABLE
1 one-pound can tomatoes with liquid

Chop tomatoes and stir into skillet. Add the pork and tomato mixture to the sauerkraut in the casserole. Cover and put back in the oven. Cook 1–1½ hours or until pork is fork tender. Check during cooking; if stew needs liquid, add more chicken broth. It should be thick but not dry.

Tip pot, skim off fat, check and correct seasoning.

ADDITIONAL SEASONING
2 tablespoons gin

Stir in gin if juniper berries have not been used, or put it in anyway.

For later serving, cool with lid askew so stew will not continue cooking. When cool, refrigerate. To reheat, remove any hardened fat from surface, bring stew to room temperature, and place in preheated 325° oven for 30–45 minutes, or until stew is just bubbling and warmed through.

TO FINISH
½–1 cup sour cream

Stir in sour cream and heat to warm through but not to boil.

GARNISHES
2 teaspoons grated lemon rind
2 pimientos, chopped

Sprinkle grated lemon rind over stew. Strew pimientos on top.

This stew can be reheated even with the sour cream in it.

Sweet and Pungent Pork

cook in:

1½ qt.

for sauce

3-4 qt.

for pork
combine and serve in:

3-4 qt.

Stews are an excellent introduction to a nation's cuisine because they emphasize a country's materials, methods, and way with flavors. The Chinese make a point of contrasting textures and tastes, matters not emphasized enough in the West. Serve this stew with rice.

Fresh ginger is what makes this dish distinctive; it is not as good made with candied or dried ginger. The Chinese Sweet and Sour Pickles* called for in this recipe must be made at least one full week ahead, but store-bought gherkins are an adequate substitute.

For a Western contrast, a first course might well be Braised Endive* sprinkled with diced ham. It is delicious with a Sylvaner or sparkling Vouvray, either of which will also taste good with pork. Its sweet and sour flavor will fight the wine, but the battle is an interesting one, although you might want to serve tea for the easily startled.

Hot gingerbread, with whipped cream or with tart applesauce over which lemon rind has been grated, would be a nice change from the usual fortune cookies and pineapple cubes served in Chinese restaurants.

Turn on oven to 325°.

MEAT

3 pounds boned shoulder of pork or pork loin, in 1½-inch cubes

Dry the meat on paper towels. It won't brown if it is damp.

FAT
    2–4 tablespoons light
      cooking oil, more if
      needed

Heat the oil in a skillet, and brown the pieces of pork well on all sides, a few at a time. As they are done, remove them to a lidded 3- or 4-quart ovenware casserole, preferably enameled ironware.

SEASONING
    2 teaspoons salt

When the meat is all in the casserole, stir in the salt. Cover and place in the 325° oven and allow to cook for 1 hour.

While the meat is cooking, prepare the sauce, which will be combined later with the meat.

POT VEGETABLES
    4 medium carrots, in ¾-
      inch diagonal slices
    2 medium yellow onions,
      each cut in 8 wedges
    1½ inch fresh ginger,
      peeled and sliced very
      thinly across the grain

Prepare the vegetables and place in a 1½- or 2-quart lidded saucepan, preferably enamelware.

LIQUIDS
    2 cups tomato juice
    ⅓ cup cider vinegar
    ⅓ cup juice from 2 cups of
      your own Sweet and
      Sour Pickles* or from 2
      cups sweet gherkins
      (reserve the pickles for
      later)

Add the tomato juice. Cover and simmer on top of the stove for 45 minutes. Add the vinegar and juice from the pickles. Cook 15 minutes more or until carrots are cooked but still firm.

SWEETENING
    ¼–⅓ cup granulated sugar

Add ¼ cup sugar and adjust sweetness by adding more to taste.

THICKENING
    4 teaspoons cornstarch

Remove ½ cup of the sauce and allow to cool. Add the cornstarch to it, blend until smooth, and stir into the sauce in the saucepan.

ADDITIONAL SEASONING
½ teaspoon salt

Add salt. At this point, the meat in the oven and the sauce and vegetables on top of the stove will each have cooked about an hour. Pour fat off pork, or remove with a bulb baster. Combine ingredients in the casserole. Cover and place in the oven at 325°. Turn down to 300° or whatever temperature will maintain a simmer. Cook 20–30 minutes or until pork is done.

ADDED VEGETABLES
2 cups Chinese Sweet and Sour Pickles,* or sweet gherkins in ½-inch pieces
2 green peppers, seeded and cut in 1-inch squares

Add the pickles and green peppers. Cook 10 minutes longer.

For later serving, cool and cover casserole. To reheat, place, covered, in a preheated 325° oven for 30–45 minutes, after bringing to room temperature if it has been refrigerated.

Lion's Head

for 3–4   about 1 hour to cook

cook in:

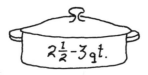

2½–3 qt.

serve in same

Lion's Head is a Chinese family dish of pork meatballs with greens. It seems to be as ubiquitous as Ireland's lamb stew or New England's corned beef and cabbage. Its succulence comes from the hand-chopped pork and its tantalizing taste from the ginger, which must be the fresh kind. (See p. 232 for sources.) It is not difficult to chop the pork; the French achieve the same superb texture for steak haché, the chef beating a tattoo on the block with a knife in each hand. There seems to be a lot of fat in the meatballs but somehow they don't turn out overly fatty. When the Chinese prepare this dish they use fat and lean, half and half.

The flowery white wines of the Rhineland are delicious with Chinese dishes; so are chilled dry Sherries or beer. (F. T. Cheng, the former Ambassador to the Court of St. James's and author of *Musings of a Chinese Gourmet,* often served Scotch and soda to Europeans who had not developed a taste for green tea.) Hard Italian salami or slivers of ham on unsalted crackers make a good first course. Serve them with a bowl of crisp raw vegetables—radishes, cauliflower buds, strips of endive, even fennel. Plain boiled rice is the only accompaniment needed for the stew. Lichee nuts are a traditional dessert, but the taste of lemon is a happy contrast—in a pie, tarts, or sherbet. Champagne is delicious with such a dessert.

MEATBALLS

2 pounds boneless pork shoulder, ⅔ lean, ⅓ fat

3 slices fresh ginger, peeled and minced very fine

2 scallions, with green, chopped

¼ cup soy sauce

¼ cup water

2 tablespoons Amontillado Sherry

¼ cup cornstarch

FAT

2 tablespoons cooking oil

Slice the pork thinly, cut the slices into narrow strips, cut the strips crosswise into dice, then chop into a coarse mince.

With your hands, mix the ginger and scallions into the minced pork.

In a separate bowl, mix the soy sauce, water, and Sherry. Then blend in the cornstarch until it is smooth. Add the mixture to the pork and mix thoroughly. At first it seems too wet, but as you blend, the pork absorbs the liquid.

Form gently into fat 2-inch patties; do not pack too firmly. If possible, refrigerate 1 hour before browning. (This is not essential.)

Heat a skillet and pour in the oil. Brown the meat patties carefully all over. As they are done, remove them to a heavy, lidded flameproof pot.

LIQUID
2½ cups canned chicken stock, or enough to barely cover (about 2 cans)

Add the chicken stock to barely cover.

SEASONINGS
1 tablespoon soy sauce
1 teaspoon sugar

Add the seasonings. Taste, and add more soy sauce and sugar if you like, but remember that the meatballs are well salted with soy sauce. Bring to a simmer, cover, and simmer 50 minutes, checking occasionally to make sure the liquid is still covering the meat patties. Skim off fat.

THICKENING
2 tablespoons cornstarch mixed with ¼ cup cold water

Add the cornstarch mixture; cook 1 or 2 minutes until sauce thickens.

For later serving, allow to cool, and refrigerate. To reheat, bring slowly to a simmer after removing any hardened fat from the surface.

ADDED VEGETABLE
4 cups Chinese cabbage (1 bunch), or 4 cups spinach (1 pound)

If you are able to get Chinese cabbage, wash well, remove first layer of tough leaves, and discard them. Cut the cabbage in quarters; cut off hard ends; cut the quarters cross-wise in ½-inch strips. Add to the pot, cover, and cook 10 minutes.

If spinach is used, wash, remove bad leaves and stems, add without chopping to pot. Cover and cook 5 minutes. Serve from the casserole, no garnish is required.

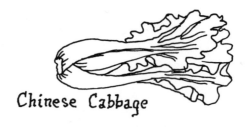

Chinese Cabbage

Chicken

Coq au Vin Rouge

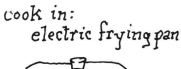

cook in:
electric frying pan

or 11"–12" skillet

serve in:

9"x 12"

for 4–5   35–40 minutes to cook
2 hours for stock to cook

Coq au Vin can be sinfully bad or sinfully good. The difference is in the quality of the chicken and the care taken in the cooking. This famous French stew, flamed with Cognac, cooked in red wine and stock, and finished with mushrooms, can be turned into Coq au Vin Riesling by the use of the flowery white wine of the Rhineland. This recipe calls for a cut-up roasting chicken and a stock made of the wing tips, neck, trimmings, and giblets. The stock is strained, then used with red wine to make the stew. A frying chicken and canned stock will do instead, but the result will not be quite as good. Since there is plenty of liquid in this stew, it can be made on top of the stove or in an electric frying pan.

Coq au Vin can be made with simple Beaujolais or California Mountain Red, but a better wine—perhaps a Burgundy bearing a town name, like Gevrey-Chambertin—means a better stew. In any event, the wine used in cooking is a good one to serve with the dish.

A first course might offer a contrast in taste and texture.

Try ham wrapped around slivers of Cheddar, with watercress, served with a chilled dry Fino Sherry or a white wine like Meursault or California Pinot Chardonnay. A simple green salad could precede the cheese course, and it could be followed by a dessert of French pastry, then coffee and Cognac.

CHICKEN
> 1 five-pound roasting chicken with giblets

Disjoint the chicken and cut into serving pieces, or have the butcher do it, but save the giblets. Cut off the wing tips. Wipe and dry the chicken pieces and set them aside.

STOCK
> Giblets, neck, wing tips
> 1 carrot, cut in half
> 1 medium onion, halved
> 1 celery stalk, cut in half
> Water to cover (about 6 cups)
> 1 teaspoon salt
> 4 or 5 whole peppercorns
> ½ teaspoon thyme
> 3 parsley sprigs
> 1 bay leaf

Wash the giblets and place them with the wing tips, the neck, and any scraps from the chicken into a 3- or 4-quart saucepan or kettle.

Add the vegetables, washed but not peeled (they will be strained out later). Cover well with water, bring to a boil, then simmer. Skim off scum as it appears, for 5–10 minutes.

When no more skimming is required, add seasonings. (If they had been added earlier, they would have been skimmed off.) Simmer 2 hours, periodically adding water to keep solids barely covered. Strain, discard solids, skim off fat. Cook down to about 2 cups; reserve.

FATS
> 2 tablespoons butter
> 2 tablespoons oil, more if needed
> 2 slices lean bacon, finely diced

In a deep, lidded 12-inch skillet or electric frying pan heat the butter and oil. Lightly cook the bacon until just golden, not crisp. Remove with a slotted spoon and reserve. Dry the chicken pieces again, brown them carefully, a few pieces at a time, pushing them to the side of the pan as they are done. Use more oil if necessary. Turn heat very low. Spread out chicken in pan.

THICKENING
2 tablespoons flour

FLAMING
¼ cup Cognac, warmed

SEASONINGS
1 teaspoon salt
¼ teaspoon pepper
½ teaspoon thyme
1 small bay leaf
2 tablespoons finely
chopped fresh parsley
2 cloves garlic, minced

LIQUIDS
2 cups dry red wine, Côte
de Beaune Villages or
Santenay
Chicken stock just to
cover (about 2 cups) or
2 cups canned chicken
broth

ADDITIONAL THICKENING
(optional)
2 tablespoons flour mixed
with ¼ cup cold water

Sprinkle flour on the chicken, turning with a wooden spoon to distribute it evenly. Cook until flour disappears.

Warm the Cognac in a small saucepan. Hold a match over it and carefully ignite. Pour the flaming Cognac over the chicken and stand well back. Shake the skillet for a few seconds until flame subsides.

Sprinkle the chicken with salt and pepper, on all sides. Add the rest of the seasonings and the bacon.

Add the wine to the skillet; add the stock to just cover. Bring to a simmer. Cover; simmer on very low flame 25–30 minutes. If any of the chicken is tender in less time, remove it and keep it warm. When all the chicken is done, remove to a warm baking dish.

Cook the liquid in the skillet at a fairly high heat for about 10 minutes to reduce it about half.

Remove bay leaf, tip pan, and skim off fat. If sauce is too thin for your taste, thicken it with flour mixed into a thin paste with cold water and cook until sauce thickens. Check and correct seasoning, then pour sauce over the chicken.

For later serving, cool, cover the baking dish well with foil, and refrigerate. To reheat, bring to room temperature. Place in preheated 325° oven for 30–40 minutes or until it is just warmed through.

GARNISHES

½ pound button mush-
rooms, or larger ones,
sliced

2 tablespoons butter

Salt and pepper

¼ cup finely chopped
parsley

Lightly sauté the mushrooms in butter. Salt and pepper them and scatter over the chicken. Sprinkle parsley over all.

Chicken Tarragon

for 4–6   ¾–1 hour to cook

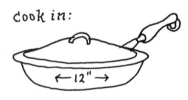

cook in:

← 12″ →

serve in:

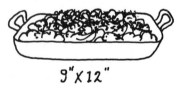

9″ X 12″

The French traditionally use fresh tarragon to stuff a chicken, which imparts full flavor. Its use here shows how subtly the herb can flavor a dish.

This chicken is excellent with rice and a side dish of quickly cooked peas and cauliflower. A light and flowery white wine of the Loire, such as a Pouilly-Fumé or Sancerre, or a Chenin Blanc or Gray Riesling from California would be appropriate. A crisp salad of endive and watercress or spinach could provide a subtle contrast, followed by a selection of goat cheeses served with crusty bread and a fruity red wine from the Rhône or Burgundy's Côte de Beaune—a Hermitage or Volnay. Dessert might be a dacquoise or fruit tart, if there's a good bakery in the neighborhood, or, for a sharper note, fresh pineapple and cookies.

CHICKEN

2 frying chickens, dis-
jointed

Dry the chicken pieces on paper towels. They won't brown if they are wet.

FAT
  4–5 tablespoons clarified
    butter

In a large heavy skillet with a lid brown the chicken on all sides in the hot clarified butter. (To clarify butter, heat ¼ pound in a small saucepan until it foams but does not brown. Skim off the foam, and pour the clear butter off the sediment in the bottom. It is the milky solids which make the butter burn quickly. Clarified butter left over can be saved for another time. See p. 235 for clarifying butter in quantity.)

POT VEGETABLE
  ¼ cup chopped shallots, or
    ¼ cup chopped white
    part of scallions and 1
    small garlic clove,
    minced

Add the shallots and cook until they are soft but not brown.

Turn down flame under skillet.

SEASONINGS
  1 teaspoon salt
  ½ teaspoon pepper
  ¼ teaspoon dried tarragon
  ½ teaspoon thyme
  1 bay leaf
  1 tablespoon finely
    chopped parsley

Sprinkle seasonings over the chicken. Stir in carefully.

THICKENING
  2 tablespoons flour

Sprinkle in flour and stir until it disappears.

LIQUIDS
  ½ cup dry Vermouth
  Hot chicken broth, as
    needed

Add the dry Vermouth, scraping the pan to loosen any bits stuck to the bottom.

Cover pan, and turn heat to a point that will maintain a simmer. Cook for 20 minutes, checking occasionally to see if more liquid is needed. Add hot chicken broth if stew gets too dry. When the breasts are done, remove and keep warm. Cook the rest another 25 minutes, or until tender. Put the breasts back in pot to warm up, then allow the liquid to cook down until there is about ½ cup. Check seasoning.

TO FINISH
½ cup heavy cream

For immediate serving, remove chicken to a hot baking dish. Stir cream into the contents of the skillet, and heat but do not boil. Pour over the chicken.

To serve later omit cream, allow to cool in the baking dish; cover with foil.

To reheat, bring dish to room temperature, then place in a preheated 325° oven for 30 minutes. Add cream and heat 5 minutes more.

GARNISH
4 tablespoons chopped fresh parsley

Sprinkle parsley over the chicken.

Mediterranean Chicken

for 4–6   about 1½ hours to cook

Green olives and mushrooms give a summery Riviera look to this elegant chicken with its smooth and slightly piquant sauce. It is adapted from a recipe developed by Leon Lianides for his Coach House restaurant in New York City; he thinks the sauce is better when strained. The dish can be

cook in a 4 qt.
flameproof casserole

serve in:

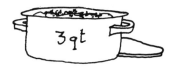

3 qt

FAT
2 tablespoons olive oil

POT VEGETABLES
½ cup finely chopped onion
1 cup diced leeks, white
   part only
2 pounds (4 cups) fresh
   ripe tomatoes, coarsely
   chopped
3 garlic cloves, unpeeled
2 small chili peppers,
   chopped, or ⅛ teaspoon
   crushed red pepper

LIQUIDS
2 cups boiling canned
   chicken broth
2 cups white wine,
   Pouilly-Fumé or Côte
   de Provence

made without straining the sauce, in which case the tomatoes and the garlic should be peeled and finely chopped.

A crisp wine like Pouilly-Fumé or a Côtes de Provence complements the chicken, but a fruity red like the Juliénas or Chiroubles of Beaujolais would also serve well. A fine first course would be Jambon Persillé.* Plain rice is probably the best accompaniment for the chicken, followed by a lettuce and watercress salad, and some goat cheese or a mild Fontina. Dessert could be Pears in Red Wine.*

In a heavy, lidded flameproof pot (not cast iron or aluminum; they affect the taste of the tomatoes) heat the olive oil.

Slowly cook the onions and leeks, turning with a wooden spoon until they are soft but not brown—about 10 minutes.

Add the tomatoes and garlic, cover pot, and cook on a low flame 10 minutes for the tomatoes to render their juice. Add the chili peppers. The sauce will be strained, hence the peeling of the tomatoes and garlic is unnecessary.

Add the chicken broth, then the wine, and bring to a simmer.

SEASONINGS
½ teaspoon thyme
½ teaspoon basil
½ teaspoon orégano
½ teaspoon dill
2-inch piece of orange
  peel
1 teaspoon salt
4–5 grinds of the pepper-
  mill
A good pinch of saffron

CHICKEN
4 leg-and-thigh sections,
  disjointed
2 whole breasts, split

ADDITIONAL FATS
2 tablespoons butter
2 tablespoons olive oil

ADDED VEGETABLE
½ pound small white mush-
  rooms, sprinkled with
  lemon juice and sautéed
  lightly

TO FINISH
½ cup pitted olives
2 tablespoons lemon juice
Tabasco

Add the seasonings, except saffron; simmer uncovered 45 minutes.

Strain the sauce, pressing through as much as possible. Allow it to cool slightly and degrease; the oil forms a film that is easy to remove.

Return the sauce to the original pot, bring to a boil. Boil vigorously to reduce the sauce to one third. Correct the seasoning and add the saffron.

Dry the chicken on paper towels. It won't brown if it is wet.

In a heavy skillet, heat the butter and oil and brown the chicken lightly. Add the dark meat (legs and thighs) to the simmering sauce. Cover and cook 10 minutes.

Add the white meat (breasts) and the mushrooms. Cook 15 minutes, or until chicken is tender.

For later serving, set the lid of the pot askew and allow stew to cool, then cover and refrigerate. To reheat, bring to room temperature, place, partially covered, in preheated 325ᶜ oven for about 30 minutes, until the chicken is just warmed through. It is essential not to overcook the chicken.

Add the olives, lemon juice, and several dashes of Tabasco. Sprinkle with parsley.

Chicken Cacciatore

cook in:

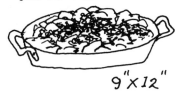

3–4 qt.

serve in:

9" x 12"

This dish may be popular because of its romantic name—chicken stewed the hunter's way, in oil, with wine and seasonings. Onions, garlic, and tomatoes are inevitable ingredients; rosemary, basil, cinnamon, and allspice, occasional ones. This version calls for orégano, basil, bay, and red wine. White wine, Vermouth, Marsala, or various Sherries could be used instead (the last three with water or broth). A good companion for the stew would be a Risotto* containing ham or bacon and maybe some olives and green peppers.

The wine you choose for cooking, perhaps a Chianti or Valpolicella, is also good for drinking with the stew. Italian sausage is a fine first course, and a nice salad might be a plate of broccoli flowerets and raw mushrooms, marinated in French dressing. Some soft Italian cheeses and ripe apples and pears would make a good dessert.

Turn on oven to 325°.

In a heavy skillet, heat the oil.

FAT
¼ cup olive oil, more if needed

Cook the onions slowly in the oil until they are limp and golden. Remove them with a slotted spoon to a heavy, lidded casserole. (Do not use an iron vessel unless it is enameled because the tomatoes—to be added later—will take on a metallic taste.)

POT VEGETABLE
3 medium onions, chopped

4 chopped slices of bacon

CHICKEN
2 frying chickens, dis-jointed, breasts split

Dry the chicken pieces and brown them in the skillet, a few at a time, using more oil if necessary. As they are browned, add them to the casserole.

SEASONINGS

1 teaspoon salt
Several grinds of the peppermill
2 garlic cloves, minced
½ teaspoon dried basil
½ teaspoon dried orégano
1 bay leaf

Sprinkle salt and pepper on the chicken and stir thoroughly. More salt and pepper may be needed later. Sprinkle in the rest of the seasonings. Use more basil or orégano, or both, if you want more of their taste.

LIQUIDS

2 cups Italian canned tomatoes, undrained
½ cup dry red wine, Valpolicella or Chianti
Hot canned chicken broth, if needed during cooking

1/28 oz Progresso Crushed Tomatoes c̄ added Purée

Add the tomatoes and wine. In this case the tomatoes constitute most of the liquid for the stew, as well as being a pot vegetable. Hot chicken stock can be added in small quantities during cooking if the chicken gets too dry. Bring to a simmer, cover, and place in the oven at 300° or whatever temperature will just maintain a simmer.

Cook 40–60 minutes, or until chicken is fork tender. Tip pot and skim off fat. Check and correct seasoning.

For later serving, cool with lid askew to prevent further cooking. Cover and refrigerate. To reheat, bring stew to room temperature, then place in preheated 325° oven for 30 minutes or until stew is just bubbling or warmed through.

TO FINISH

1 green pepper, in 2-by-¼-inch strips
1 tablespoon olive oil

Sauté green pepper lightly in oil and scatter over the chicken.

Chicken Paprikash

for 6–8 about ¾ hour to cook

1.20.87
• excellent
• good company dish

Putting paprika in a stew is supposed to make it Hungarian, but most of the time the paprika is so old and flat that it does little more than color the stew. Good paprika adds an

cook in:

3-4 qt.

serve in same, or

9" x 12"

incomparable redolence, which is just what you want. True chicken paprikash is made with lard and lots of onions, but the taste of lard is out of favor with Americans, so we have not used it in this version. Caraway and tomatoes round out the flavor. Sweet cream sometimes replaces sour cream; the two can be combined; or cream can be dispensed with altogether, depending on the richness desired. The liquid can be water, tomatoes and their juices, chicken stock alone or with wine, or any combination. A paprikash is a repertoire in itself; you can extend its range even further by varying the starch accompaniment—noodles, spätzle, Butter Dumplings,* boiled potatoes go equally well.

This paprikash is superb with the flowery green-white wines of Austria or the fruitier whites of the Rhine, though some people prefer it with the big rough reds from Hungary. A grand first course is a variety of smoked sausages or salamis, particularly Hungarian kielbasa, or you could try a version of Antipasto* or an Hors d'Oeuvre Varié,* served with licorice-flavored Raki or Pernod.

A leafy lettuce salad with oil and vinegar might precede some hard and salty cheese, and the dessert should be a miraculous Viennese pastry *mit Schlag:* apple strudel lost under the whipped cream, for instance. Finish it off with icy Slivovitz, Kirsch, or Poire, and black coffee.

FATS
2 tablespoons butter
2 tablespoons cooking oil, more if needed

Turn on oven to 325°.

In a heavy skillet, heat the butter and oil.

POT VEGETABLE
3 medium onions, thinly sliced

Cook the onions until golden but not brown. With a slotted spoon remove them to a flameproof lidded casserole.

CHICKEN
2 frying chickens, disjointed, breasts split

Disjoint the chickens, split the breasts, and wipe dry. In the skillet, brown the chicken pieces, removing them to the casserole as they are done.

SEASONINGS
2 tablespoons sweet Hungarian paprika
1 teaspoon caraway seeds, crushed
1 teaspoon salt
5 or 6 grinds of the peppermill

Sprinkle the seasonings over the contents of the casserole; stir carefully to spread throughout. Hungarian paprika should be used here.

LIQUIDS
1 can chicken broth
½ cup dry white wine, California Chablis or Riesling
2 tablespoons tomato paste

Mix together the broth, wine, and tomato paste. Add to the casserole. Bring to a simmer. Cover and place in the oven at 325°. Turn down to 300° or whatever temperature will just maintain a simmer.

Cook about 30 minutes or until chicken is fork tender. Tip pot and skim off fat. For later serving, cool with lid askew. Cover and refrigerate. To reheat, remove any hardened fat from the surface, bring to room temperature, and place in preheated 325° oven for 30 minutes.

TO FINISH
1 cup sour cream

Remove the chicken from the sauce. Keep warm. Stir sour cream into the sauce. Return the chicken to the sauce, and heat but do not boil.

GARNISH
1 green pepper in ½-by-2-inch strips
1 tablespoon butter

Lightly sauté the green pepper in the butter. Sprinkle over the chicken.

Rabbit

Lapin aux Prunes

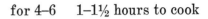

for 4–6   1–1½ hours to cook

cook in:

4 qt.

serve in:

9"X12"

Rabbit seems to have disappeared from American cuisine. Natives who were delighted to come and try other stews being tested for this book refused our invitation for rabbit, and we had to fall back on our international acquaintances. The result is this single stew. For Hasenpfeffer, Civet, and the rest, the epicure must seek elsewhere. The rabbit is marinated in well-seasoned red wine with a lacing of vinegar, then browned with shallots and cooked in Bordeaux. The fruit is added, and the rabbit is finished with its liver and currant jelly—a Belgian masterpiece. The marinade is discarded because it has a gamy taste and a lot of oil, but if you can learn to like it, strain and use the marinade in the cooking. The French and Belgians do.

St. Emilion with fur, Médoc with feathers, say the English about clarets to serve with game. Gastronomes of Bordeaux are apt to use minor château bottlings from either district for the cooking and a finer bottle at least ten years old for drinking with this dish.

A first course might be a game pâté or a Jambon Persillé* with a white Graves. For salad try endive and watercress with a sharp dressing. Cheese should be the best Brie or Camembert you can find, served with a still grander, older château bottling. An excellent fruit tart sets the stage for coffee and a fine Armagnac, Marc, or Cognac.

RABBIT
1 three-to-four-pound
  rabbit cut in pieces

Trim liver and reserve. Wipe rabbit pieces with damp paper towel.

MARINADE
Tops of 2 stalks celery
2 sprigs parsley
½ teaspoon thyme
1 bay leaf
1 clove garlic, unpeeled,
  smashed with the flat of
  a heavy knife
2 medium onions, quar-
  tered
1 teaspoon salt
8 whole peppercorns
½ cup wine vinegar
½ cup olive oil
1 cup dry red wine, Cali-
  fornia Pinot Noir or
  Beaune

Place the marinade ingredients in a nonmetallic bowl, add the rabbit, cover, and refrigerate for 24 hours. Stir occasionally.

FRUITS
1 cup pitted prunes
½ cup dried apples
½ cup seedless raisins
  Boiling water

One hour before beginning to cook the rabbit, put the fruit in a bowl and cover with boiling water.

Drain the rabbit, discarding marinade (unless you like the gamy taste). Dry the rabbit thoroughly on paper towels for browning. It won't brown if it is damp.
Turn on oven to 325°.
In a heavy skillet, heat the butter and oil.

FAT
2 tablespoons butter
2 tablespoons olive oil

POT VEGETABLE
¼ cup chopped shallots

Slowly cook the shallots until they are limp, not brown. Remove with a slotted spoon to a 3½-quart lidded flameproof casserole. In the skillet, brown the rabbit pieces, a few at a time, removing them to the casserole as they are done. Turn heat on very low under the casserole.

THICKENING
3 tablespoons flour

Sprinkle the flour in, a little at a time, stirring and turning the rabbit until the flour disappears.

LIQUID
1 tablespoon wine vinegar
About 1 bottle dry red
  Bordeaux wine

Add the vinegar, and gradually add the wine to almost cover, stirring to incorporate the flour and to detach any bits stuck to the bottom.

SEASONINGS
4 or 5 parsley stems
1 clove garlic, unpeeled,
  flattened with the flat of
  a heavy knife
½ teaspoon thyme
1 teaspoon salt

Put the parsley stems, garlic, and thyme into a bag made of a double layer of cheesecloth, and tie it with white thread. Press into the middle of the stew. Add the salt.

Drain the fruit, then stir into the stew. Bring to a simmer, cover, and place in the oven at 300° or whatever temperature will just maintain the simmer. Cook 1–1½ hours or until rabbit is tender.

Tip pot and skim off fat.

TO FINISH
The liver of the rabbit
2 tablespoons currant
  jelly

Sauté the liver briefly in butter, then mash it with a fork, discarding any fibers that won't mash. Stir into the stew. Stir in the jelly.

For later serving, cool and refrigerate. To reheat, bring to room temperature, place in a preheated 325° oven for 30 minutes or until stew is just bubbling and warmed through.

GARNISH
¼ cup finely chopped
  fresh parsley

Sprinkle with parsley.

Fish

Sailors' Stew

cook in:

3 qt.

serve in bowls

FISH
3 pounds firm-fleshed salt-water fish, such as cod, eel, squid, haddock, sea bass, halibut, etc.

This unusual fish stew calls for browned fish—as many kinds as possible—simmered in a well-reduced wine stock. If the fish are cooked with their bones, the stew is heartier.

A sharp, dry Muscadet in the cooking and with the dish would also taste good with a first course of oysters on the half shell or cold shrimp with mayonnaise. Good French or Italian bread goes with the stew, either as it comes, or as some form of garlic bread.

You might follow the stew with a salad of cucumbers and tomatoes dressed with oil and vinegar and sprinkled with chives or dill. Fresh fruit or ice cream with a splash of liqueur would make a light dessert.

Wash the fish and cut it into 2-inch pieces. Peel the eel. Clean the squid; chop it in small pieces. A good fish merchant will do this for you. Boning is a matter of taste, but the fish loses a lot of its identity when it is boned, and it is harder to brown. None of these fish have the myriads of tiny bones that shad or bluefish do. If you do have the fish boned, more fat may be needed for browning.

STOCK:

LIQUIDS
   1 bottle dry white wine,
      Muscadet, or a white
      Burgundy like Pinot
      Chardonnay
   4 cups water

VEGETABLES
   2 cloves garlic, chopped
   ¼ cup chopped shallots
   2 medium onions, chopped

SEASONINGS
   1 medium onion, stuck
      with 3 whole cloves
   ½ teaspoon thyme
   ¼ teaspoon tarragon
   1 bay leaf
   3 sprigs parsley
   ½ teaspoon salt
   ½ teaspoon pepper

THICKENING
   2 tablespoons butter
   2 tablespoons flour

FATS
   4 tablespoons olive oil
   4 tablespoons butter

Pour the wine and water into a deep kettle or saucepan.

Add the vegetables. If shallots are unavailable, use ¼ cup chopped white of scallions and another small garlic clove. The stock will be strained later.

Add the seasonings. Since the stock is to be boiled down, be careful with salt.

Bring to a boil; simmer over a very low flame for 1 hour or until liquid is reduced by one third.

Strain the stock. Mix the butter and flour with fork or fingers, stir into stock, and cook 2–3 minutes until it thickens. Pour into a 3-quart flameproof casserole, preferably a wide shallow one, which can be brought to the table.

In a skillet, heat the oil and butter and lightly brown the fish in this order: eel, squid, halibut, bass, haddock, cod. As they are browned remove them to paper towels to drain. When fish is all browned, add to the stock, bring to a simmer, and simmer on a very low flame for 20 minutes or until fish is tender. Check seasoning.

As with most fish dishes, this tastes best when served immediately, but the stock can be made ahead and the fish browned, ready for the 20 minutes of cooking together.

GARNISHES
Thin lemon slices
¼ cup finely chopped fresh
parsley

Lay lemon slices over the stew, sprinkle with parsley. Serve in bowls or soup plates.

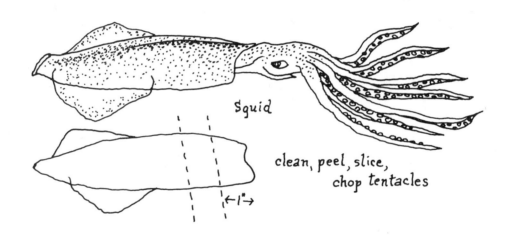

Squid

clean, peel, slice,
chop tentacles

←1″→

Oxtails

Ökörfarok Ragú

cook and serve in:

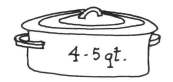

4 - 5 qt.

MEAT
2 oxtails, disjointed, or 4 pounds packaged oxtails (3–4 sections per person)

Every country seems to make a rich stew of oxtails. This Hungarian version with the strange name has an extra savor from the paprika and the novel arrangement of its added vegetables. Like most stews, it lends itself nicely to cooking ahead of time.

A hearty red wine like a fruity young Beaujolais or a fuller, older Rhône wine like a Châteauneuf-du-Pape or Hermitage is a good companion for this dish. A first course might be a pâté or terrine, because there isn't a great deal of meat on the oxtails. After the stew try a sheep cheese like Greek Feta or a Brie or Camembert. Salad is scarcely necessary with so many vegetables. Fresh fruit would be a fine dessert —a bowl of cherries, or pears, or peaches—although you might want to use the dish's Hungarian origin as an excuse for serving Viennese pastry with lots of whipped cream. Very cold plum brandy, Slivovitz, could come with coffee.

Turn on oven to 325°.

Dry oxtails for browning. They won't brown if they are damp.

FAT
 4 tablespoons cooking oil,
 more if needed

In a large skillet, heat the fat and brown the pieces of oxtail, a few at a time, removing them as they are done to a lidded flameproof casserole. Turn the heat on very low under the casserole.

THICKENING
 2 tablespoons flour

Sprinkle the flour on the meat and stir until it is absorbed.

SEASONINGS
 2 teaspoons salt
 2 cloves garlic, minced
 2 tablespoons Hungarian
 paprika
 ½ teaspoon freshly ground
 black pepper

On a saucer mash together the garlic and salt with a strong fork. Add with the other seasonings to the meat. Medium Hungarian paprika is best.

POT VEGETABLES
 1 medium onion, chopped
 2 ripe tomatoes, peeled
 and chopped, or 1 one-
 pound can tomatoes

Stir in the onion, then the tomatoes with their juice.

LIQUIDS
 1 cup canned beef broth
 ½ cup dry red wine

Add broth and wine and stir carefully to unstick the bits from the bottom of the casserole. Cover and place in 325° oven. Turn down to 300° or whatever temperature will just maintain a simmer. Cook 2–2½ hours or until meat is almost coming off the bones. During cooking stir and check for dryness, adding small amounts of water if needed. The stew should be rather thick. Tip pot, skim off fat; check and correct seasoning. Remove the stew to a clean casserole or baking dish large enough to accommodate the added vegetables.

ADDED VEGETABLES

16 scallions, with green,
  coarsely chopped
¾ pound large mushrooms,
  sliced
6 medium carrots, diced
  in ½-inch cubes
2 cups potatoes, cut in
  1-inch cubes

GARNISHES

¼ cup finely chopped fresh
  parsley
2 whole pimientos,
  chopped

Arrange the vegetables around the meat, keeping each kind in its own section. Sprinkle lightly with salt and pepper.

Cover with lid or foil. Return to oven and cook 30–45 minutes more, or until meat and vegetables are tender.

For later serving, allow to cool with lid askew, then cover and refrigerate. To reheat, bring to room temperature and place in preheated 325° oven for 30–45 minutes or until stew is just bubbling and warmed thoroughly.

Sprinkle with parsley and pimientos.

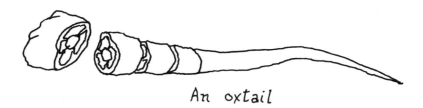

An oxtail

Vegetable

Ratatouille I

cook in:

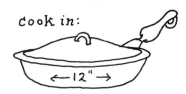

←12"→

serve in a bowl or:

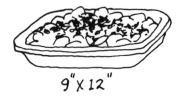

9" × 12"

FAT
4 tablespoons olive oil,
more as needed

You need big pots for this redolent Mediterranean delight of eggplant and zucchini, green pepper and tomatoes, onion and garlic and herbs. Although it is not a main course, it is hard to make just a little, since the best blend of flavors comes from making a lot. Ratatouille is marvelous with roasts and *grillades,* particularly lamb, and delicious as a cold first course, with crusty bread. A bottle of fruity red wine like Chiroubles or Juliénas from the Beaujolais district or a white wine like Muscadet or Pinot Chardonnay Mâcon suits it nicely. Like all country dishes, it can vary enormously, depending on the taste of the cook and the availability of vegetables. Enthusiasts divide in two camps, some preferring a dry Ratatouille, others a wet one. Here is a wet version; a dry one follows. Both are excellent. Try the dry one with a stew, the moist version with a roast.

In a large heavy, lidded 11- or 12-inch skillet, 2½ inches deep (preferably enameled ironware), or shallow 2½- or 3-quart lidded flameproof casserole heat the oil.

VEGETABLES

2 large yellow onions,
   coarsely chopped
2 medium green peppers,
   coarsely chopped
2 cloves garlic, minced
1 medium eggplant
2 medium zucchini
4 cups (1 two-pound can)
   Italian tomatoes,
   undrained

Cook the onions, green peppers, and garlic slowly until they are tender but not brown. Turn off heat while other vegetables are prepared. Wash the eggplant, cut off the stem, cut in 1-inch cubes. Peeling is not necessary.

Wash and lightly scrape the zucchinis, cut off ends, cut in ½-inch slices.

In another skillet, heat more olive oil. Quickly, on high heat, sauté the eggplant and zucchini, a few pieces at a time, about 1 minute on each side. (This will require more oil; the eggplant soaks it up.) As each batch is finished, transfer it to the skillet with the onions and peppers. Add the tomatoes to the other vegetables.

SEASONINGS

1½ teaspoons salt
¼ teaspoon freshly ground
   pepper
1 teaspoon dried
   orégano
1 teaspoon dried basil
1 bay leaf
½ cup finely chopped fresh
   parsley

Add the seasonings and stir to mix thoroughly. Bring to a simmer. Cover and cook 45–60 minutes over a very low flame, as low as possible, until zucchini and eggplant are tender but not too mushy. Check and correct seasonings, adding any extra salt, pepper, or herbs in small quantities to taste. For later serving, cool and refrigerate. To reheat, bring slowly to a simmer, and simmer just to heat through. It can also be served cold.

GARNISH

¼ cup finely chopped fresh
   parsley

Sprinkle with parsley.

Ratatouille II

cook and serve in:

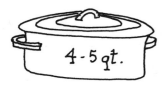

4-5 qt.

VEGETABLES
2 or 3 small eggplants
3 or 4 small zucchinis
2 large onions, sliced
2 medium green peppers,
   sliced
3 cloves garlic, minced
4 cups (1 two-pound can)
   Italian plum tomatoes,
   drained
2 tablespoons tomato
   paste

FAT
4 tablespoons olive oil,
   more as needed

The dry version of ratatouille is particularly delicious served cold. It is a refreshing first course when eaten by itself, or spread on bread, or served with slices of Hungarian or Polish sausage. Hot, it is a good accompaniment for a pork roast or chops, for a simply cooked chicken dish, for veal. It is excellent for a buffet—as relish, vegetable, or salad—hot or cold.

Wash the eggplants, remove ends, cut in ½-inch slices. If slices are very unequal in size, cut the larger ones in half. Peeling is not necessary. Wash and lightly scrape the zucchinis, remove ends, and cut in ½-inch slices.

Note: Large eggplants and zucchinis will have more moisture. To extract it, place the sliced vegetables in a bowl, sprinkle them with salt, put a weight on top and let stand for 30–60 minutes. Drain; wash and dry each piece. Cut the eggplant so that slices of it are about the same size as zucchini slices.

In a heavy skillet, heat the oil and quickly sauté the eggplant and zucchini slices, a minute on each side, removing them as they are done to a bowl or plate. (More oil will be needed; the eggplant soaks it up.) In the same skillet, heat more oil (4 tablespoons). Slowly cook the onions, peppers, and garlic until they are tender but not brown. Add the drained tomatoes mixed with the tomato paste.

SEASONINGS
1 teaspoon salt
¼ teaspoon freshly ground
black pepper
1 teaspoon dried
orégano
1 teaspoon dried basil
1 bay leaf, crumbled
½ cup finely chopped fresh
parsley
Salt and pepper for
sprinkling

Add the seasonings except the last. Stir carefully to mix well. Check and correct seasoning.

Turn on oven to 325°.

In the bottom of a heavy, lidded 4- or 5-quart casserole put ⅓ of the tomato mixture. Next add a layer of ½ of the eggplant and zucchini. Sprinkle lightly with salt and pepper. Put ½ of the remaining tomatoes on top, then the rest of the eggplant and zucchini, salt and pepper; finish with the last of the tomatoes.

Cover and place in preheated 325° oven for 45–60 minutes, or until vegetables are tender. Check occasionally. Tip pot and baste with the juices. If it appears too moist, leave cover off for a while. It can be served either hot or cold. For later serving, cool and refrigerate. To reheat, bring to room temperature, place in preheated 325° oven for 30–45 minutes, until it is just bubbling and warmed through.

GARNISH
¼ cup finely chopped fresh
parsley

Sprinkle with parsley.

Unbrowned Stews

Beef

Basic Unbrowned Beef Stew

for 6–8   3–3¼ hours to cook

cook in:

5–6 qt.

serve in bowls, from the pot or a tureen

This simple, hearty stew appears all over the world in slightly different forms. The variations and additions—rice, pasta, beans, sausage, spices, and vegetables—depend on the cuisine of the country and the changes of season. An important ingredient, no matter how simple or exotic the stew, is salt. Even this very elementary version is a delight, its good, beefy taste enhanced by the vegetables, so long as there is enough salt. To see what can happen to this stew, add a Spanish chorizo sausage or Polish Kielbasy for the last half hour of cooking.

Beer matches it well; so does a good, cold rosé like a Tavel, or a red wine like a Beaujolais, a Chianti, or a California Gamay. Because it is a meal in itself, it hardly needs a first course, perhaps only crisp vegetables to accompany cocktails.

Neither salad nor cheese is necessary. The best dessert is a bowl of fruit or a good ice cream or sherbet and cookies.

MEAT
3–4 pounds boned shank
or shin of beef, in 2-inch
pieces
2 pounds beef bones

Trim off outside fat. Wash the meat and bones.

LIQUID
Water to cover completely

Place the meat and bones in a large heavy pot on the top of the stove. Cover with water, and bring to a boil. Skim off the scum as it appears on the surface. Boil gently until no more scum appears—15–20 minutes.

POT VEGETABLE
4 onions, sliced coarsely

Add the onions.

SEASONINGS
2 teaspoons salt
½ teaspoon freshly ground
black pepper
1 bay leaf

Add the seasonings. More salt may be needed later when the vegetables are added. The seasonings are added after skimming so they won't be skimmed off.

Adjust the heat to maintain a simmer. Cook partially covered for about 2½ hours, or until the meat is tender. Skim off any fat as it appears on the surface—it is easier to remove before the vegetables go in. Add more water as the liquid boils down, if needed to keep the meat and bones covered. When the meat is tender, discard the bones.

COLORING (optional)
1 tablespoon meat color-
ing, as unflavored as
possible

Add the meat coloring to avoid the gray look of boiled meat.

ADDED VEGETABLES
1 cup coarsely chopped
   celery
6–8 medium potatoes,
   peeled and halved
1 small rutabaga (yellow
   turnip), quartered and
   sliced ½ inch thick
2 green peppers, coarsely
   chopped

Tip the pot and remove grease. Add the vegetables; add the peppers 10 minutes after the others. Bring to a boil again, and adjust the flame to maintain a simmer. Cover and cook ½ to ¾ hour more, or until vegetables are tender. Check again for salt; potatoes absorb some. If needed, add by ½ teaspoons until broth is to your taste. If by any chance it is too salty, add water.

For immediate serving, transfer the stew carefully to a clean casserole or heated soup tureen. Serve in deep bowls or soup plates.

To serve at a later time, leave in the original pot; cool with lid askew. When cool, refrigerate. To reheat, remove hardened fat from the surface, bring to room temperature, and slowly bring to a simmer. Simmer 5 minutes, just to heat through.

TO FINISH
1 package frozen peas,
   cooked
½ cup finely chopped fresh
   parsley

Add the peas and parsley.

Collops

for 6   about 1–1½ hours to cook

cook in:

2½ qt.

Collops is the early English word for slices of meat, and versions of this stew—thinly sliced beef very well seasoned —surely delighted Chaucer. It calls for a rather moist accompanying vegetable, creamed onions or mashed turnips perhaps, and a leafy green salad.

Serve in:

8" × 10"

Instead of a first course, you might serve dishes of almonds, cheese, shrimp, ham, and olives—the sort of thing the Spanish call *tapas*—with cold Manzanilla or Fino Sherry, white Port or Sercial Madeira. Beer is better than wine with the collops, although a Gewürztraminer from Alsace or a dry Amontillado Sherry might be pleasant. Since there is no starch except the toast served with the stew, fresh fruit and cake, such as angel food, would not be too heavy a dessert.

MEAT
   3 pounds top round of
     beef in thin slices

Buy a 3-pound top round beef roast and cut it in ⅜-inch slices. Trim fat. Pound the beef slices flat. Place them in a Dutch oven or heavy lidded casserole and add the seasonings. (Very little salt is required at this time because salty anchovies and canned broth will be added later.)

SEASONINGS
   ½ teaspoon salt
   2 or 3 grinds of the
     peppermill
   A pinch thyme
   A pinch marjoram
   A pinch savory

LIQUIDS
   2 cups canned beef broth
   Hot water if needed to
     barely cover

Add the liquid. Add hot water if necessary during cooking to keep the liquid to about 2 cups.

POT VEGETABLE
   1 onion, chopped

Add the onion.

Cover and simmer 1–1½ hours or until meat is tender, either in a 325° oven or on the top of the stove. In either case adjust the heat to just maintain a simmer.

6 anchovies, coarsely
   chopped
¼ cup dried bread crumbs
1 tablespoon butter

To serve immediately, remove the slices of meat and arrange them in overlapping layers on a warm platter or baking dish. Strain the sauce and add the anchovies and bread crumbs. Simmer until slightly thickened. Stir in butter. Check and correct seasoning. Pour the sauce over the meat slices.

To serve later, cover the ovenware platter or baking dish lightly with foil; when cool, cover well and refrigerate. To reheat, allow it to come to room temperature and place in a preheated 325° oven for 30 minutes.

GARNISHES
   Toast triangles
   1 thinly sliced lemon
   1 tablespoon capers
   2 tablespoons finely
      chopped fresh parsley

Surround the meat with toast triangles, arrange the sliced lemon over the top, and sprinkle with capers and parsley.

Pot-au-Feu

for 6–8   3–3½ hours to cook

Pot-au-Feu isn't a stew at all: it's a weekly French dinner. Housewives buy the beef, the turnips, and the leeks as regularly as the sun rises. The basic recipe never varies. The beef is cooked in a chunk, then cut up for serving; the pot vegetables are discarded after they have flavored the stock; new vegetables are added and served with the beef. There are occasional additions—Polish sausage; a trussed chicken; a butt, bone, or hock of ham—all tied to the pot handle with a string so they can be hauled up from the depths and tested for doneness. When they are done (the sausage may take half an hour, the chicken an hour, the ham two), they are removed and kept warm in a dish with a cup of the broth, to

cook in:

Serve soup in bowls,
meat and vegetables
on a platter.

be returned to the pot for reheating during the last ten minutes. The soup is served first, and then the meat and vegetables, with gherkins and a little mound of coarse salt on the side of the plate: two courses from one pot. Red wine comes from the grocery, bought by the degree of alcohol it contains, *onze* or *douze pour cent*. Youngsters get an inch in a glass, with water.

For a first course there may be a bit of sausage with bread, some radishes with butter, or some leftover Ratatouille.* The cheese is whatever there is, but there is certainly a bowl of fruit in season: pears or peaches; some strawberries to be picked up by the stem and dipped in powdered sugar; perhaps a bunch of grapes. If there are no tarts from the pâtisserie, there's a Crème Caramel. With the coffee, there is Marc or Calvados or Cognac, depending on what's in the house and whether the family hails from Burgundy or Normandy or the Loire. A simple meal. Every week. No reason to change it.

MEATS
4 pounds rump, boneless chuck roast, or fresh brisket of beef
2 pounds beef bones
1 veal knuckle, cracked

Wash the meat and bones; trim fat from meat; place meat with the bones in a large (5- or 6-quart) kettle.

POT VEGETABLES
1 large onion stuck with 3 whole cloves
2 medium carrots
2 medium white turnips

Peel the onion; trim off ends. Clean the carrots and turnips and cut them in half. They are to flavor the stock and do not need to be peeled. They will be strained out later. Add the vegetables to the kettle.

LIQUID
Water to cover

Cover completely with water.

SEASONINGS
2 teaspoons salt
½ teaspoon thyme
1 bay leaf
2 parsley sprigs
1 teaspoon freshly ground
    pepper

Add the salt. Bring to a boil; reduce to a simmer. Skim off scum as it appears on the surface. After 10–15 minutes, or when no more skimming is necessary, add the rest of the seasonings. They are added later so that they won't be skimmed off.

Simmer very slowly, partly covered, adding water occasionally to keep everything covered. Start testing the beef after 2½ hours of cooking. When it is fork tender, turn off heat, and remove meat. Drain stock through a colander, reserving the liquid and discarding the vegetables and bones. For a richer stock, put the liquid back in the pot, turn on heat and boil to reduce by about one quarter to one third. Turn heat down to a simmer.

Skim off fat, check seasoning, adding salt and pepper to taste. Return the meat to the pot.

ADDED VEGETABLES
8 medium carrots
8 medium potatoes
4–8 leeks (optional) 1
    inch in diameter, white
    part only
4 medium onions
6 white turnips
1 one-pound yellow turnip

Scrape the carrots, cut in quarters lengthwise. Peel and halve the potatoes. Halve the leeks (if used) and wash thoroughly. Cut the onions into quarters. Peel and halve the white turnips; peel the yellow turnip and cut in ¾-inch cubes. (The idea is to have all the vegetables cooked in the same time. If the potatoes are large, they may need to be quartered; if the onions are large, cut them into eighths.) Add the vegetables to the kettle. Bring to a simmer, cover, and cook 20–30 minutes, or until vegetables are tender. Skim off fat if necessary. Season to taste.

COLORING (optional)
1 tablespoon meat coloring, as unflavored as possible

Add meat coloring if desired.

For later serving, allow to cool thoroughly, partially covered, and refrigerate. Remove any hardened fat from the surface. To reheat, bring slowly to a simmer on the top of the stove and simmer just to heat through, not to cook further.

½ cup finely chopped fresh
parsley

Serve the soup in bowls, the beef on a platter surrounded by the vegetables. Or serve slices of beef with soup and vegetables in large shallow soup plates. In either case, sprinkle liberally with parsley.

Daube de Boeuf à la Provençale

for 8   2–2½ hours to cook

cook in:

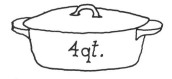

4 qt.

Serve in same

A *daube* is the same as an *estouffade,* that is, a smothered stew cooked without much liquid. Its name comes from the *daubière* it used to be cooked in, an oval pot with a flat, tight-fitting lid on which coals were heaped, much like a Western chuck-wagon bean pot. A *daube* in the Provence style calls for white wine. In one region nearer the Rhône, they use the red wine of Châteauneuf-du-Pape, which we prefer. Anchovies, even capers, are added to the Riviera *daube.*

This is a hearty dish which really needs no accompaniment but bread or plain rice and lots of wine of the Côtes de Provence, red or white, or California Mountain Red or White. The first course might be an Antipasto,* the salad a green one, the cheese salty Chèvre. Ice cream with fresh fruit would be a good dessert, with chilled Kirsch and black coffee.

MEAT
4 pounds boned shoulder, chuck fillet, or chuck center cut of beef, in 2-by-2-by-1-inch pieces

Trim off the fat. Wipe the pieces with damp paper towels.

MARINADE
1½ cups dry red wine
⅓ cup Cognac
3 tablespoons olive oil
2 stalks celery, coarsely chopped
6 medium carrots in ½-inch slices
2 medium onions in ¼-inch slices
2 cloves garlic, minced
2 teaspoons salt
½ teaspoon black pepper
1 teaspoon thyme
1 large bay leaf, broken
2 tablespoons finely chopped fresh parsley

FAT
8 slices lean bacon, blanched

THICKENING
Sifted flour on a plate (about ½ cup)

ADDITIONAL SEASONINGS
½ teaspoon salt
¼ teaspoon pepper

Place the beef in a large, nonmetallic bowl with the marinade ingredients. Cover and allow to stand for at least 3 hours, stirring from time to time.

Blanch the bacon by simmering it in 2 quarts water for 5 minutes. (This will keep it from overwhelming the other flavors.) Drain, rinse, and dry it with paper towels; cut strips in half. Line the bottom of a heavy flameproof casserole with half the bacon. The pot should have a well-fitting lid. The French make a paste of flour and water and seal the lid on with it for the long slow cooking.

Turn on oven to 325°.

Drain the beef and vegetables, reserving the liquid. Pick out the pieces of beef, sprinkle with salt and pepper and roll them in flour, shaking off excess as you go along. Arrange them close together in a layer over the bacon. (You should have enough for at least one more layer, depending on the diameter of the pot.)

POT VEGETABLES
    1 pound mushrooms,
        coarsely sliced
    2 cups drained Italian
        canned tomatoes (2 one-
        pound cans)
    20–24 black pitted olives
        (one 3⅞-ounce can,
        drained)

Mix the pot vegetables with the marinade vegetables; strew some of the mixture over the meat. Make as many layers of alternating meat and vegetables as possible, ending with vegetables. Then lay on the rest of the bacon.

LIQUIDS
    The marinade liquid
    Canned beef broth, if nec-
        essary to barely cover

Add the liquids; bring to a boil on top of the stove. Reduce to a simmer, cover, and place in the oven at 325° or whatever temperature will maintain the merest simmer. Cook 2–2½ hours or until beef is tender. Remove from the oven, tip pot, and skim off fat. Stir, and check seasoning.

For later serving, allow to cool with lid askew so the stew will not cook further in its own heat. Cover, and refrigerate.

To reheat, bring to room temperature; place in preheated 325° oven for 30–45 minutes, or until stew is just bubbling.

GARNISHES
    10 flat anchovy fillets,
        chopped (optional)
    ½ cup finely chopped fresh
        parsley
    4 pimientos in ½-inch
        squares

For an extra Provençale touch, sprinkle with anchovies. Garnish with parsley and pimientos.

Russian Beef Borscht

cook in:

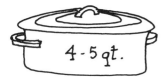

4-5 qt.

serve in:

Soup mugs or bowls and

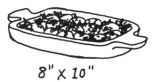

8" X 10"

Beef Borscht is a glorious and traditional dish in both Russian and Jewish cuisines. As with Pot-au-Feu, the soup is served first, followed by the beef and vegetables. This is a shortened version of the traditional method; the balancing of sweet and sour has been carefully worked out for this book by Fanny Engle, author of the delightful *Jewish Festival Cookbook*. We have substituted canned beef broth for her stock made with flanken. She also often uses one piece of fresh brisket, which she slices and serves with potatoes after a first course of the soup. Chunks of shank are used here so the Borscht could be served all together in bowls— soup, meat, beets, and potatoes—as a single course.

The soup is served with sour cream; the meat is served with horseradish, pickles, and boiled potatoes. Broccoli* is a good side dish and a simple red wine such as a Beaujolais would be appropriate. For dessert have a strudel or some other Viennese or Russian pastry. Strong tea in glasses, with lemon, is traditional, but coffee is served as frequently as not.

MEATS
2 pounds boneless shank or shin of beef in 2-inch pieces
1 marrow bone
1 beef knuckle bone

Trim as much fat as possible from the beef. Wash and drain the meat and bones and place in a 4-quart lidded flameproof casserole or kettle.

POT VEGETABLE
2 medium onions, quartered

Add the onions.

LIQUIDS

3 one-pound cans beef
  broth (about 6 cups)
2 cups tomato juice
Juice from 1-pound can
  julienne beets, the beets
  reserved

SEASONINGS

1 teaspoon salt
¼ teaspoon pepper
Juice of one lemon
1 tablespoon cider vine-
  gar
2 tablespoons brown
  sugar

TO FINISH

1 one-pound can julienne
  beets (this is the second
  can)

GARNISHES

Sour cream (optional)
6 boiled potatoes
¼ cup fresh parsley, finely
  chopped

Add the broth, bring to a boil, simmer 10–15 minutes, skimming off scum as it forms.

Add other liquids. Add water if needed to cover.

Purée (or blend in a blender or finely chop) the canned beets; reserve to add later.

Add the seasonings, bring to a boil, turn down to a simmer, cover, and simmer very slowly for 2–2½ hours or until beef is fork tender.

Remove beef to an 8-by-10-inch baking dish. Discard bones. Skim off fat from the liquid. Spoon out enough liquid to barely cover meat. What is left in the casserole is the *soup*.

Strain and add the beets to the soup.

For later serving, cover the baking dish well with foil, put soup in a container. Cool and refrigerate. Remove hardened fat on the surface of the soup before serving, hot or cold.

To reheat stew, remove the hardened fat from the surface, bring to room temperature, place in a preheated 325° oven for 30 minutes, or until stew is just bubbling and warmed through.

Heat the beets and liquid from the second can. Add the liquid to the *soup* and spread the beets on the stew in the baking dish.

Put a dollop of sour cream (if used) on each bowl of soup, hot or cold.

Serve the stew with boiled potatoes.

Sprinkle parsley on everything.

Wienersaft Gulyàs

cook in:

4-5 qt.

serve in:

9" X 12"

Goulash Vienna style keeps to Hungarian tradition by cooking beef and onions with paprika and caraway. However, the Viennese prefer oil or butter to lard for the browning and they like to add tomato paste, garlic, and lemon rind, a bow to strong Italian influence. The dish is usually served with Noodles,* but Balkan spätzle, Butter Dumplings,* Italian gnocchi, or Risotto* is also good with it. In any case, it absolutely requires fresh Hungarian paprika or at least the kind labeled Hungarian paprika which is found in specialty food shops.

A flowery white wine, like an Austrian Riesling or Muller-Thurgau from Loiben or Krems, is good with this; so are hearty reds like Egri Bikaver from Hungary or a French Rhône. Lettuce salad with cucumbers is a good accompaniment, followed by some strong cheeses. A Viennese dish is always an excuse to have something *mit Schlag.* If you don't feel like torte or pastry, have the whipped cream with berries of the season, Viennese coffee, and Kirsch.

MEAT
2 pounds boneless chuck fillet, boned shoulder, or cross rib of beef, in 1½-inch cubes

Turn on oven to 325°.

Wipe and dry meat on paper towels. It is not to be browned, but needs to be dry anyway.

SEASONINGS
2 teaspoons marjoram
2 teaspoons lemon rind, finely chopped
1 teaspoon caraway seeds
1 clove garlic, minced
1½ teaspoons salt

Crush or mash together all the seasonings.

FAT
    4 tablespoons butter

POT VEGETABLE
    2 pounds onions, chopped

ADDITIONAL SEASONINGS
    2 tablespoons sweet Hungarian paprika
    1 tablespoon tomato paste

THICKENING
    2 tablespoons flour

LIQUID
    1–2 cups hot water

In a heavy, lidded flameproof casserole melt the butter. Add the mashed-together seasonings.

Add the onions and cook gently until they are limp and transparent, not brown.

Sprinkle in the paprika. Stir to mix and cook for about 1 minute. Stir in the tomato paste. Add the beef, maintaining a very low flame under the casserole. Stir until the meat is coated (not browned) and loses its own red color.

Sprinkle flour over the stew; stir until it is absorbed.

Add enough water to cover the bottom of the casserole well. The meat and onions supply their own liquid. Bring to a simmer, cover and place in the oven at 325° or at whatever temperature will just maintain the simmer. Cook 1½–2 hours or until beef is tender. Check occasionally during cooking. If stew is dry and in danger of sticking or burning, carefully add hot water ½ cup at a time—the stew is supposed to be thick. When beef is tender, tip pot and skim off fat. Check and correct seasonings.

For serving at this time remove to a clean casserole or warm baking dish if the cooking vessel looks messy.

For later serving, allow to cool partially covered, cover the casserole or seal the baking dish with foil, and refrigerate. To reheat, return to room temperature, and place in a preheated 325° oven for 30–45 minutes or until stew is just bubbling.

1 green pepper in 2-by-¼-
    inch strips
1 tablespoon butter
2 whole pimientos,
    chopped
10–12 black olives (Greek
    olives if possible)

Lightly sauté green pepper in butter until tender but still firm. Sprinkle over the stew with pimientos and olives.

Puchero Criolla

for 6–8   2½–3 hours to cook

cook in:

5-6 qt.

1½ qt.

serve as 2 courses

9" x 12"
or all together in
large soup plates.

When Puchero moved to South America from the Iberian Peninsula it was greatly improved by the addition of squash and lots more beef. We use shank or shin beef, but other cuts can be used—flanken (the boned strips at the end of a rib roast or under the shoulder) or boned brisket (the first part of the breast next to the shank). It is accompanied by a separate casserole of garbanzo beans (chick peas), tender cabbage, and chorizo sausage, which can be made at the same time.

Puchero is usually served all together, in soup plates; but the broth can be served as a first course, along with glasses of chilled Manzanilla or Fino Sherry, followed by the meat and vegetables and a South American red wine, a California Zinfandel, or a Gamay Beaujolais. There is really no need for a salad or a separate cheese course. A South American dessert is creamed quince, Dulce de Membrillo, served with Münster or Bel Paese and Ruby Port, but a melon with some Port poured in its hollow is lighter and more refreshing.

MEAT
3 pounds boneless beef shank or shin in 2–3-inch pieces
(Flanken or fresh brisket can be used instead. The brisket can be cooked in one piece and sliced for serving, or cooked in large serving pieces.)
2 pounds beef bones

LIQUID
Boiling water to cover, 3–4 quarts

SEASONINGS
1 tablespoon salt
6 whole peppercorns
2 cloves garlic, chopped
1 bay leaf

POT VEGETABLES
2 celery stalks, with tops
3 sprigs parsley
2 carrots, halved lengthwise
1 or 2 leeks

Wash beef and bones and place in a 5- or 6-quart deep kettle.

Pour boiling water into kettle to cover the meat and bones thoroughly. Bring to a boil; boil gently 10–15 minutes, skimming off scum as it appears. When no more scum is forming, turn down to a simmer.

Add seasonings. They are added after skimming so they won't be skimmed off.

The vegetables should be washed, but the carrots need not be peeled. They are for flavoring the stock and will be strained out. Add them to the kettle.

Bring to a boil; turn down to a simmer and simmer partially covered for 2–3 hours, or until meat is just tender.

Drain, reserving liquid. Discard vegetables and bones, after extracting marrow from the latter, if you like. (Marrow can be spread on toast and sprinkled with salt and pepper for a little hors d'oeuvre.) Skim off fat from liquid; check and correct seasoning to taste; put the beef back in; bring back to a simmer. Remove ½ cup liquid for bean casserole.

ADDED VEGETABLES
2 small acorn squash
6 medium potatoes
6 white turnips
2 green peppers (op-
tional)

Wash all the vegetables. Quarter the squash, and remove seeds, but do not peel. Peel and quarter the potatoes; peel and halve the turnips; trim, seed, and coarsely chop the peppers (if used). Add the vegetables to the stew, peppers 10 minutes later than the rest. Cover and simmer 20–30 minutes or until vegetables are just tender.

Serve in soup plates with the garbanzo-bean casserole as a side dish.

For serving at a later time, it is best to refrigerate or even freeze the meat and stock without the vegetables. When you reheat, bring the pot to a simmer and add the vegetables 20–30 minutes before serving.

GARBANZO-BEAN CASSEROLE
½ small cabbage, cored (about 1 pound), in 8 wedges
½ cup reserved stew liquid
1 one-pound-four-ounce can chick peas (gar-banzo beans), drained
½ pound chorizo sausage, sliced
¼ teaspoon freshly ground black pepper

Place the cabbage in a 1½- or 2-quart lidded flameproof casserole. Add the reserved stew liquid. Cover and cook 5–10 minutes until cabbage is just tender. Add the chick peas, sausage, and pepper. Bring to a boil, turn down to simmer, cover, and simmer on very low flame 10–15 minutes. Serve as a side dish with the Puchero Criolla.

To serve later, cool and refrigerate. To reheat, bring to room temperature, then place in preheated 325° oven for about 30 minutes. Moisten the bean dish with more stock if it is too dry.

GARNISH
½ cup finely chopped fresh parsley

Sprinkle parsley on everything.

cook in:

2½ qt.

serve in:

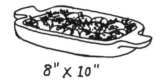

8" X 10"

Every family has a dish passed down from Grandma. She never remembers where it came from but it is certainly not from any cookbook. The origin of this stew with its surprising ingredient, cherry jam, is unknown. The recipe is remembered from childhood by a New Englander with a Swedish background to whom it was known as Armenian stew, because it seemed, homehow, Middle Eastern. It is not quite like the Swedish meatballs called Frikadeller. It has an attractive reddish-brown color, and is easy to prepare, requiring no browning. Furthermore, its taste changes in a most delightful way, depending on the size of the meatballs.

Crisp raw vegetables with a sharp dip (p. 201) are a good first course, with Martinis or cold Akvavit, in memory of grandmother. Fettuccine, white and buttery, is a good companion for the stew, followed by a lettuce and endive salad, and some mild Scandinavian cheese. For wine have the dry fresh white of the Loire, Muscadet. Fresh Fruit* with a liqueur is a perfect light dessert.

MEATBALLS
1½ pounds ground chuck
1 teaspoon salt
3 or 4 grinds of the peppermill

Mix the ground beef with the salt and pepper, using your hands to spread the seasonings evenly through the meat. Form into 1-inch balls. Place the meatballs in a heavy, lidded nonmetallic casserole.

LIQUIDS
1 eight-ounce can tomato sauce
Juice of one lemon
1½ tablespoons cherry jam
Hot water, if needed

Mix the liquids together and pour over the meatballs. Bring to a simmer.

1 bay leaf
1 teaspoon grated lemon rind

Add the seasonings.

Cover and cook ¾ hour on a very low flame, shaking the pot or stirring occasionally to keep from sticking. If the liquid cooks down too much, add small amounts of hot water to keep it from becoming too dry. Degrease if necessary by tipping the pot and blotting up the fat with a paper towel.

If the dish is to be refrigerated, allow it to cool first. To reheat, remove any hardened fat from the surface, bring slowly to a simmer, and cook just long enough to heat through.

GARNISH
Small sprigs of fresh parsley

Stick little sprigs of parsley in among the meatballs.

Five Fragrances Beef

for 6   1½–2 hours to cook

cook in:

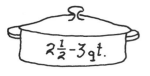

2½–3 qt.

serve in same

Five fragrances is a wondrous blend of spices which is available in Chinese groceries. (See p. 232 for sources.) This dish cannot be attempted without it. It is strangely delicate in flavor and should be served with rice, and green beans or Chinese Broccoli.*

A fish or seafood course is a hearty preface to this dish, a Hot Chicken Consommé* with thin slices of bamboo shoot and chopped chives a lighter one. Chilled dry Sherry, even the ultra-dry Manzanilla, is delicious with the stew, although tea or hot rice wine is closer to tradition. Lime sherbet with a touch of liqueur and a sprinkling of something crisp (see p. 230) is a cooling finale.

FATS
2 tablespoons cooking oil
½ teaspoon sesame oil

SEASONINGS
1 teaspoon salt
3 slices peeled fresh
ginger
2 cloves garlic, crushed
3 tablespoons sugar
1 teaspoon monosodium
glutamate
½ teaspoon cracked black
pepper
1 teaspoon five fragrances
spice, ground
3 tablespoons white vine-
gar
¼ cup soy sauce

MEAT
3 pounds boneless chuck
or top or bottom round
of beef in 1½-inch cubes
(buy in one piece and
cube it later)

POT VEGETABLE
3 whole scallions, including green

LIQUIDS
Water to barely cover
Hot water during cook-
ing, if needed

Turn on oven to 325°.

Heat a heavy, lidded casserole or Dutch oven and put in the oils.

Add the salt, stir, and turn heat to medium. Add the ginger and garlic; stir-fry until golden, not brown.

Remove pot from stove.

Mix the rest of the seasonings together and add to the casserole.

Trim off fat and cut beef into cubes. If you are going to use chopsticks make cubes a little smaller, 1 inch instead of 1½ inches.

Add the beef to the casserole.

Add the scallions. They can be left whole, because they will be strained out.

Add water to barely cover the meat. Bring to a boil; reduce to a simmer; cover; place in the oven at 300° or whatever temperature will just maintain the simmer. Cover and cook 1½–2 hours, or until beef is fork tender. Check during cooking; add hot water if necessary to keep stew from sticking.

Remove meat from liquid and place it in a clean casserole. Strain the liquid into a saucepan; skim off fat.

THICKENING
2 tablespoons cornstarch, mixed with ¼ cup cold water

Add the cornstarch mixture to the liquid; cook 1 or 2 minutes until it thickens.

Add Sherry and bring to a simmer.

Pour over the meat in the clean casserole.

ADDED SEASONING
2 tablespoons Fino or Amontillado Sherry

For later serving, allow to cool with lid askew before refrigerating. To reheat, remove any hardened fat from the surface and bring slowly to a simmer. Simmer just to heat through.

TO FINISH

If the liquid is too thin, add more cornstarch mixed with water, 1 teaspoon at a time, until it is the thickness you want. Cook 1–2 minutes after each addition. The sauce should not completely cover the meat. If there is an excess, serve it on a bowl, or save it to warm up with any leftover stew.

GARNISH
4 scallions, green only

Cut the green part of the scallions across in ¼-inch slices, to make little rings of green. Sprinkle over the stew.

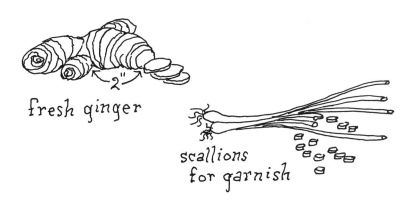

fresh ginger

scallions for garnish

Veal

Lemon Veal

for 4–5   1¼–1½ hours to cook

cook in:

4-5 qt.

serve in:

9" X 12"

Veal and lemon are a perfect combination, and this tangy stew, sparked with cayenne and Worcestershire, is wonderfully light. The recipe calls for chicken broth; homemade veal stock would be more delicate, in which case white wine should be used in place of the Vermouth. Serve it with rice or noodles, preferably vermicelli or green fettuccine.

This sprightly stew calls for a good wine—a ten-year-old Pomerol or Graves, a full, rich Hermitage or Côte Rôtie, a fine Barolo or Chianti. The dish has an Italian savor, and an Antipasto* could well precede it, although Francophiles might prefer Hors d'Oeuvre Varié,* accompanied by a Pouilly-Fuissé or Pouilly-Fumé. Instead of a salad, a separate course of braised celery or of asparagus with Hollandaise would be excellent. Fontina or Taleggio would be good for a cheese course, and rich Italian pastry a good dessert, but a big bowl of cherries, followed by a fine Kirsch and coffee, would be best of all.

MEAT
  3 pounds boneless veal shoulder in 1½-inch cubes

FATS
  1 tablespoon butter
  1 tablespoon oil
  2 slices bacon, diced

SEASONINGS
  ½ teaspoon marjoram
  ¼ teaspoon cayenne
  1 teaspoon salt

THICKENING
  3 tablespoons flour
  ½ cup cold water

LIQUIDS
  1 can (13-ounce) chicken broth
  ¼ cup dry Vermouth

COLORING
  1 teaspoon meat coloring, as unflavored as possible

ADDITIONAL SEASONINGS
  1 bay leaf
  1 clove garlic, minced
  2 teaspoons Worcestershire sauce
  6 quarter-inch slices lemon

Turn on oven to 325°.

Trim fat from veal, dry in paper towels. The meat is not to be browned but it still needs to be dry.

In a lidded flameproof casserole, melt the butter, add the oil, and slowly cook the bacon until it is golden brown. Add the meat, turning and cooking on low heat until it loses its color but does not brown.

Sprinkle with the seasonings, stir and cook 5 minutes on the same low flame.

Mix the flour and water to a smooth paste.

In a saucepan heat the chicken broth, add the thickening, stir into the casserole. Add the Vermouth.

Stir in the coloring.

Add the seasonings, laying the lemon slices on top. Bring to a boil, then turn down to a simmer.

Cover and place in preheated 325° oven. Turn down to 300° or whatever temperature will just maintain the simmer. Cook for 1–½ hours or until the veal is fork tender.

Tip pot and skim off fat. Remove bay leaf and lemon. Turn into a warm 9-by-12-inch baking dish.

ADDED VEGETABLE
  1 package frozen
    artichoke hearts,
    cooked, or 1 arti-
    choke hearts, drained

Add the artichoke hearts; cover the dish well with foil.

For immediate serving, put the foil-covered baking dish in the oven for 10 minutes to heat through.

For later serving, cool, lightly covered with foil. When it is thoroughly cooled, seal with the foil and refrigerate.

TO FINISH (optional)
  ½ cup heavy cream

To reheat, bring to room temperature, and place in pre-heated 325° oven for 30–40 minutes, or until stew is just bubbling and warmed through. Stir in heavy cream, if used.

GARNISHES
  6 thin lemon slices
  ¼ cup chopped fresh dill
    or 1 teaspoon dried dill

Put lemon slices in a row on the stew; sprinkle dill over everything.

Blanquette de Veau

for 4–6   1½–2 hours to cook

cook in:

4-5 qt.

then:

3 qt.

Serve in same, or
9" x 12" baking dish

This is the classic white stew of *la cuisine bourgeoise,* and French housewives pride themselves on keeping it as white as possible, blanching the veal, using white pepper, being sure the butter doesn't brown, picking the whitest mushrooms and bleaching them whiter still with lemon juice and carefully finishing the dish with egg yolks and cream. All the care makes blanquette sound difficult, but it isn't. Variations are casual: an onion stuck with cloves, a carrot, cooking in wine and chicken stock. One French friend will have none of these, even resisting a final grating of nutmeg. Her blanquette is white and delicate, served with plain rice, preceded by a country pâté or Jambon Persillé.* The salad is garden lettuce or endive, the cheese whatever looks good in the shop, and the wine Châteauneuf-du-Pape, with a bottle of white Hermitage to start. Dessert is fruit of the season.

MEAT
    3 pounds boneless shoulder of veal in 1½-inch cubes
    Boiling water to cover

Wash veal, place in a large saucepan, and pour boiling water over it to cover. Turn flame on under the saucepan and agitate the veal with a wooden spoon until the pink disappears. Bring to a boil and allow to boil gently for 30 minutes, skimming off scum and grease as they appear. This is blanching the meat.

Turn on oven to 325°.

SEASONINGS
    2 teaspoons salt
    ½ teaspoon white pepper

Add the salt and pepper. (Seasonings are added after skimming to keep them from being skimmed off.)

Drain the meat and reserve the liquid.

FAT
    4 tablespoons butter

Melt the butter in a lidded flameproof casserole on top of the stove over a very low flame.

POT VEGETABLE
    ⅓ cup chopped shallots, or ⅓ cup chopped white part of scallions and 1 small garlic clove, minced

In the hot butter, cook the shallots until they are limp and transparent but not brown. With heat still very low, add the pieces of veal, and stir to coat the meat with butter. Do not allow to brown.

THICKENING
    4 tablespoons flour

Sprinkle flour over the contents of the casserole and stir until it disappears.

LIQUID
    Liquid reserved from the blanching, enough to barely cover

Add the liquid; it should not completely cover the meat. Mix well. Leftover liquid can be reduced and used as stock another time.

Salt and white pepper, if
needed
½ teaspoon thyme
1 bay leaf
6–8 stems fresh parsley

ADDED VEGETABLES
18–24 small white onions
1 pound small white
mushrooms
Juice of 1 lemon

TO FINISH
3 egg yolks
½ cup heavy cream
½ cup sauce from the stew

GARNISHES
Pinch of nutmeg
1 lemon, thinly sliced
2 tablespoons finely
chopped fresh parsley

Check for salt and pepper; add the rest of the seasonings, tied in a cheesecloth bag to keep the stew as free as possible of color. Parsley stems discolor the stew less than the leaves.

Cover casserole and place in a 325° oven. Cook for 30 minutes, or until veal is almost tender.

While the stew is cooking, peel the onions and make small cross cuts on the root ends to keep them from separating. Clean the mushrooms with a damp paper towel; sprinkle with lemon juice to keep them white. Add the onions and mushrooms to the stew. Cook ½–¾ hour more, or until meat and vegetables are tender.

For later serving, allow to cool. Cover, then refrigerate. To reheat, let the stew come to room temperature, and slowly bring to a simmer on top of the stove. When the stew is warmed through, beat the egg yolks with the cream; gradually add the hot sauce from the stew, stirring steadily. Stir carefully into the stew. Do not let the stew boil after adding the eggs and cream. If you want to, carefully remove the stew to a clean warm casserole or baking dish.

Sprinkle with nutmeg. Lay the lemon slices, overlapping, in a row along the center of the stew, and sprinkle with parsley.

Lamb

Irish Stew

for 4–6   about 1½ hours to cook

cook in:

4-5 qt.

serve in:

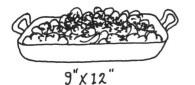

9" X 12"

Irish stew requires lots of loving care and lots of salt. The tradition is to use breast and neck of lamb, but they are too gristly for Americans. More delicate versions call for a bouquet garni, which misses the point of the stew, which should be an unctuous blending of unbrowned lamb, cabbage, and onions, thickened with potatoes. New York's St. Regis Hotel is famous for its lamb stew, which is made with leeks, a favorite seventeenth-century vegetable. When they are not to be found, a can of undiluted vichyssoise can replace an equal amount of the stewing liquid. The St. Regis blanches the lamb, then starts again with cold water, but this extra step is not necessary if you skim the first boiling with some care. Blanching is a simple process. Put the lamb in cold water, bring to a simmer for five minutes, then pour off the clouded water, rinse the meat, and start again with cold water. An equally easy way is to put the meat in tepid water, let it stand for an hour, then drain it. Many cooks find either way easier than skimming.

Boiled potatoes, string beans, and pearl onions are fine additions, although some like carrots and peas. An Irish beginning for the meal could be smoked trout or salmon. An endive and watercress salad tastes fine after the stew, followed by an Irish Cheddar or Camembert. The wine might be a dry white from the Chardonnay grape, a Meursault or Pouilly-Fuissé, a Riesling from the Rhine vineyards, or a light red claret from the Bordeaux districts of Graves or Haut Médoc. A really good apple pie could top off the meal.

MEAT
3 pounds boneless lamb shoulder in 1½-inch pieces

Wash and drain the lamb. Place in a 4-quart lidded pot on top of the stove.

LIQUID
Water to cover, 8–10 cups

Cover with cold water and bring to a gentle boil. Skim off the scum as it rises to the top, and continue skimming as long as scum reappears, for 10–15 minutes.

SEASONINGS
2 teaspoons salt, or 1 teaspoon per quart of water
½ teaspoon white pepper
1 bay leaf

When no more scum appears, add the seasonings. Turn down to the merest simmer. Simmer partially covered until meat is tender, about 1 hour.

Remove the meat to a 3- or 3½-quart casserole or 9-by-12-inch baking dish.

ADDED VEGETABLES
2 large onions, sliced
1 small head of cabbage, diced
1 cup sliced leeks, white part only (3 or 4 leeks, 1 inch in diameter or the equivalent) or 1 can vichyssoise

Check the seasoning in the liquid, skim off any grease, and add the vegetables. Split the leeks lengthwise and wash thoroughly before slicing across. If leeks are unavailable, remove the equivalent of a can of vichyssoise from the liquid, and add the vichyssoise.

Cook vegetables until just tender, 10–15 minutes. Remove the vegetables from the liquid and place on top of the meat in the casserole or baking dish.

To each 4 cups of liquid, 1 cup leftover mashed potatoes, or 1 cup instant potato flakes

Add the mashed potatoes *or* the potato flakes to the liquid; stir and cook until smooth, about 5 minutes. Check the seasoning again; potatoes absorb salt.

ADDED SEASONING
Dash of Worcestershire sauce

Stir in Worcestershire sauce. Pour over the meat and vegetables. For immediate serving cover the casserole, or wrap foil over the baking dish, and warm through in a 350° oven about 10 minutes.

For later serving allow to cool, partially covered, before covering to refrigerate.

To reheat, bring the covered casserole or foil-covered baking dish to room temperature, and place in a preheated 325° oven for about 30–45 minutes.

TO FINISH
6–8 boiled potatoes, halved
¼ cup finely chopped fresh parsley

Serve with boiled potatoes.

Sprinkle with parsley.

For later serving, the boiled potatoes can be warmed up with the stew. For this you may need a larger casserole or baking dish.

Lamb Curry

for 8   1½–2 hours to cook

In Indian stews lamb is often marinated and cooked in buttermilk with a multitude of spices. Variations are endless: Indian women grind and mix fresh spices every day to suit the dish they are to make. This recipe can be used for chicken (which takes less time to cook) or beef (which takes

cook in:

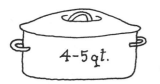

4-5 qt.

serve in smaller pot, or
9" x 12" baking dish

more). Clarified butter is essential and quite easy to prepare. Serve the curry with the traditional chutney, and Saffron Rice* or plain fluffy rice.

Curry is exotic and cries for exotic companions: a cold lobster with mayonnaise, eaten with the fingers and served with Champagne, or, for a British touch, gin and tonic; or Pimm's Cup served with dishes of salted cashews and pistachios. For dessert, a bowl of persimmons, pomegranates, or mangoes and grapes is a crowning touch. Or try bananas sautéed in butter, flamed with Triple Sec, and sprinkled with coconut and slivered almonds.

MEAT
  4 pounds boneless lamb
  shoulder in 1½-inch
  cubes

Wipe the meat with damp paper towels.
Trim off fat.

MARINADE
  2 cups buttermilk
  3 cloves garlic, smashed
  with the flat of a heavy
  knife
  1 teaspoon cooking oil

Place the lamb, buttermilk, garlic, and oil in a nonmetallic bowl. Allow to stand 1–2 hours, turning occasionally with a wooden spoon.

Turn on oven to 325°.

FAT
  5 tablespoons clarified
  butter

Clarify ½ pound butter by melting it in a small saucepan until it foams but not until it browns. Remove from heat, skim off the foam and pour the clear butter off the milky sediment in the bottom of the pan. It is the milky solids which cause butter to burn quickly. Measure out 5 tablespoons of the clear butter; save the rest to use another time. For clarifying butter in quantity see p. 235.

POT VEGETABLE
  4 medium onions,
  chopped

In a heavy, lidded flameproof casserole, heat the butter and slowly cook the onions until they are limp and transparent.

SEASONINGS

- 3 cloves garlic, chopped
- 2 teaspoons salt
- 2 teaspoons grated dried ginger
- 3½ teaspoons ground cumin
- 3½ teaspoons ground coriander
- 2 four-inch sticks cinnamon, broken in half
- 4 teaspoons turmeric
- 1½ teaspoons ground cardamom
- 6 whole cloves, broken
- 1 bay leaf
- 1 teaspoon crushed chili peppers
- ¼ teaspoon cayenne
- ½ teaspoon black pepper

THICKENING

- 2 tablespoons flour
- 2 teaspoons ground almonds (optional)
- 2 teaspoons poppy seeds (optional)

LIQUID

The buttermilk marinade, with more buttermilk added if necessary to bring quantity back to 2 cups

With a strong fork, mash the garlic with the salt on a saucer. Add to the onions.

In order not to get mixed up, line up the spices with a piece of wax paper in front of each bottle. Measure the spice and place it on the wax paper. After they are all measured, add them one by one to the casserole, stirring and blending them with the onions, and cook 2 minutes.

The last three seasonings are the ones that affect the hotness. The proportions here are for a mild curry. Check the taste later and add more hotness if you wish, or serve a little dish of each of the condiments so each person may adjust the flavor to his own taste.

Drain the lamb well; discard garlic; reserve the marinade. (It will be a little pink.) Add the lamb to the casserole, stirring to mix it well with the spices, onions, and butter, but not to brown.

Sprinkle flour on the contents of the casserole; stir until the flour is incorporated evenly. The almonds and poppy seed are also thickening agents, not essential since flour is being used.

Add the buttermilk; stir to dislodge any bits stuck to the bottom of the casserole. Bring to a simmer, cover, and place in the oven at 325° or whatever temperature will just maintain a simmer.

Cook 1½–2 hours or until lamb is fork tender. Tip pot and skim off fat. Check and correct seasoning.

Remove meat with a slotted spoon to a clean, smaller casserole or baking dish. Discard cinnamon and bay leaf.

TO FINISH
1 tablespoon flour
½ cup buttermilk

Mix the flour and buttermilk until smooth; add to the sauce in the original casserole; cook 2 minutes; pour over the meat in the clean casserole.

For later serving, allow to cool with lid askew, before refrigerating. To reheat, bring back to room temperature and place in the oven at 325° for 30 minutes.

CONDIMENTS
Chutney
Shredded coconut
Seedless raisins
Toasted slivered almonds

Surround the casserole with little dishes of condiments, to be added to taste. The possibilities are unlimited: pickles, chopped orange or lemon peel, marmalade, crumbled bacon, guava jelly, and the coconut, raisins, and almonds are just suggestions. Chutney is essential, though.

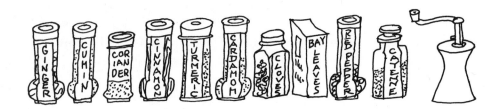

Pork

Maiale Affogato

Maiale Affogato is Italian pork stew. Literally it means drowned pork. This one is cooked, though hardly drowned, in white wine and chicken stock, with rosemary and garlic, and peppers are cooked separately and added at the end with tomatoes. If you leave out the peppers and cook a whole pork loin in Chianti, you will have Maiale Ubriacato, or drunken pork. Spaghetti with garlic and butter sauce is a fine accompaniment, although a Risotto* with ham or bacon added is also good. This stew tastes best with a white wine like Soave or Orvieto, which also suits a first course of sardines, cold boiled mussels, or clams with an herb mayonnaise. You might follow the white wine with a light red, to be finished with a selection of Italian cheeses, including Bel Paese. This dish scarcely needs a salad, although a plate of sliced cold asparagus, with sauce vinaigrette, might be pleasant on a summer's day. Fresh fruit or a fruit tart would be a satisfying dessert with Strega and coffee.

Turn on oven to 325°.

cook in:

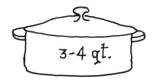

3-4 qt.

serve in same

FAT
2 tablespoons olive oil

Heat the oil in a heavy, lidded flameproof casserole. Do not use an iron vessel since it affects the taste of the tomatoes, which are added later.

2 garlic cloves, crushed
with the flat of a heavy
knife

Cook the garlic in the oil until golden but not brown; then discard it.

MEAT
3 pounds lean boneless
pork shoulder in 1-inch
cubes

Trim fat from pork. Wipe the pieces with damp paper towels.

Stir the pork into the olive oil in the casserole. Cook, stirring, for 5 minutes, not to brown, just to coat with oil and until it loses its color.

POT VEGETABLE
2 medium carrots, minced

Stir in the carrots.

SEASONINGS
2 teaspoons salt
¼ teaspoon white pepper
½ teaspoon dried rosemary, or 1 tablespoon
fresh

Sprinkle the seasonings over the contents of the casserole.

LIQUIDS
1½ cups dry white wine
1 cup canned chicken
broth

Add the liquids, stir, and bring to a simmer. Cover and place in the oven at 325° or whatever temperature will just maintain a simmer.

Cook 1½–2 hours or until the pork is tender. Tip pot and skim off fat. Check and correct seasoning.

ADDED VEGETABLES
3 green peppers in 1-inch
squares
1 tablespoon olive oil
1 can (1 pound) Italian
tomatoes, drained and
chopped, liquid re-
served

GARNISH
¼ cup finely chopped fresh
parsley, or several
sprigs of Italian pars-
ley

In a skillet lightly sauté the green peppers in the olive oil. Add to the stew. Stir in the tomatoes. Cook 15 minutes more. If the stew needs more liquid, add the tomato liquid.

For later serving, allow the casserole to cool with lid askew so it won't continue cooking. Cover and refrigerate. To reheat, bring to room temperature and place in preheated 325° oven for 30–45 minutes.

Sprinkle chopped parsley or Italian parsley leaves over the stew.

Chicken

Plain Old Chicken and Dumplings

for 6   2 hours for stock to cook
about 1 hour for chicken

cook in:

3-4 qt.

serve on a platter,

or in a tureen,
or from the pot

Anybody lucky enough to have a farm or a country grand-mother knows chicken and dumplings. This recipe calls for a stock to give a supermarket roaster the chickeny taste that comes from cooking an old bird a long time. If you are able to find a 4–5-pound stewing chicken or fowl approach-ing its first birthday, proceed instead as follows.

Cover the fowl and its giblets with 2½–3 quarts water. Fol-low the procedure for stock, skimming carefully and sim-mering for about 2 hours, or until almost tender. Remove from heat, discard pot vegetables; skim again with a cup, for there will be a lot of fat. Bring again to a simmer and add the thickening (7 tablespoons instead of 5 may be needed) and the added vegetables. Dumplings go in 20 min-utes before the stew is done, or according to the time called for by the dumpling recipe. Everything else is the same as in the recipe below. Check the stew for salt; some stews cook down more than others and the salt indicated is mini-mal. Extra pepper may be needed. To take advantage of all the lovely sauce, the old bird can be served in soup plates.

Both red and white wines complement chicken, and country cousins remember buttermilk. Smoked and salty foods taste just right beforehand: Jambon Persillé,* for instance, with a chilled dry Pouilly-Fuissé or California Chardonnay. Volnay or Châteauneuf-du-Pape goes well with the chicken, and a green salad, generous with garlic, might precede some creamy cheeses like Brie and Boursault. Pears in Red Wine* make a light dessert.

CHICKEN
   1 four-to-five-pound roasting chicken, cut in 8 pieces, with giblets
   2 pounds backs and necks

Wipe the chicken pieces with a damp paper towel; set aside. Wash giblets and extra backs and necks.

STOCK
   2 medium carrots, halved
   2 stalks celery, with tops
   2 medium onions, halved
   2 sprigs parsley
   3 quarts water
   2 teaspoons salt
   1 teaspoon white pepper

Place the giblets, backs, and necks in a deep 4- or 5-quart saucepan or kettle. Wash vegetables. There is no need to peel the carrots since the stock will be strained. Add the vegetables to the kettle.

Add the water. Bring to a boil, boil gently for 10–15 minutes, skimming off foam as it appears. When foam stops forming, add seasonings. Simmer gently for 2 hours, replacing water as it cooks away, just enough to keep solids barely covered.

Drain, discard solids, strain, and skim off fat from surface. Measure liquid. If it is more than 2 quarts (8 cups) boil vigorously to reduce to 2 quarts.

LIQUID
   The stock

Place the chicken pieces in a heavy, lidded 4-quart flameproof casserole. Pour in the stock (or 4 cans chicken broth). Bring to a simmer; skim off foam and fat as they form for 10 minutes. Cover and simmer very slowly for 30 minutes.

VEGETABLES
6 medium carrots in ½-inch slices
4 medium onions, quartered

Add the vegetables, cover, and simmer 30 minutes, or until chicken and vegetables are tender.

ADDED SEASONINGS
1 teaspoon salt
½ teaspoon freshly ground black pepper

Add salt and pepper. Tip pot, skim off fat.

THICKENING
5 tablespoons flour
½ cup cold water

Mix flour and water to a smooth paste, stir into stew, cook until it thickens, 2–3 minutes. Check and correct seasoning. Flour makes stew less salty. For a thicker sauce, add more flour, a tablespoon at a time, mixed with cold water.

For later serving, cool and refrigerate. To reheat, bring slowly to a simmer after removing hardened surface fat.

DUMPLINGS
Biscuit mix

Make dumplings according to directions on the package, but use half and half instead of milk. Dumplings should be dropped on stew that is not completely covered with liquid. If there is too much liquid, remove some for cooking the dumplings; put it back after dumplings are cooked. Cook according to instructions on biscuit-mix package. For other dumpling recipes see p. 216.

TO FINISH
½–1 cup heavy cream

Carefully remove chicken, vegetables, and dumplings to a warm baking dish or deep platter; keep warm. Bring liquid to a boil; boil vigorously for a few minutes to reduce a little. Turn heat down, add cream, heat, but do not boil. Pour over the stew.

COLORING (optional)
Yellow food coloring

Not essential, but a few drops of the coloring make the stew a handsome yellow.

GARNISHES
  2 pimientos, coarsely
    chopped
  ¼ cup finely chopped
    fresh parsley

Fricassee of Chicken

cook in:

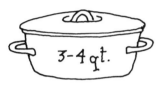

3-4 qt.

*serve in a smaller
casserole, or:*

9" X 12"

CHICKEN
  2 frying chickens, cut up

Strew pimientos on top. Sprinkle parsley over everything.

for 6   30–40 minutes

There are two schools of thought about a simple fricassee; one advocates browning, the other does not. Here is a middle course: stiffen the chicken, turning it in butter without browning. As in Blanquette de Veau, the idea is to keep the chicken as creamy-looking as possible. This recipe, a variation of Tante Marie's beautifully simple one, follows her suggestion of first blanching the chicken by letting it stand in tepid water for an hour. Mushrooms are added toward the end to lend a wisp of bouquet to the stew. The finish is classic—egg yolk, cream, and lemon juice. Rice or Butter Dumplings* go well with it.

A good fricassee calls for a delicate wine, a four- or five-year-old Burgundy from Beaune or Chambolle-Musigny, a château-bottled Graves or Médoc twice as old. First course might be a pâté, Flaming Shrimp,* or Crabmeat in Aspic,* with a three-year-old white Graves or California Sauvignon Blanc. Camembert or Brie is right for the cheese course, after an endive and watercress salad. Dessert could be French pastry or a fresh fruit dessert with a touch of liqueur.

Wash chickens.

BLANCHING
Tepid water to cover
1 teaspoon lemon juice

Place in a glass or porcelain bowl and cover with tepid (barely warm) water and lemon juice. Let stand 1 hour. This bleaches the chicken a little and, more importantly, gets rid of some of the blood, which would darken the stew.

FAT
4 tablespoons butter

Melt the butter in a heavy, lidded 4-quart flameproof casserole.

POT VEGETABLES
2 stalks celery, chopped
1 medium onion, chopped

Add the celery and onion; cook on low heat until both are limp. Do not let butter or vegetables brown. Dry the chicken with paper towels and add to the pan, turning to coat with butter and vegetables, but not to brown. Cook about 5 minutes on very low flame.

THICKENING
4 tablespoons flour

Sprinkle flour on the chicken, 1 tablespoon at a time. Turn with a wooden spoon to distribute evenly. Cook until flour disappears.

LIQUIDS
1 can chicken broth
   (about 1½ cups)
1 cup dry white wine
Hot water to barely cover

Add the liquid, stirring carefully to incorporate all the flour and clear the bottom of the pan.

SEASONINGS
1 teaspoon salt
¼ teaspoon white pepper
⅛ teaspoon cayenne
   pepper
¼ teaspoon grated nutmeg
½ teaspoon thyme
1 bay leaf
3 sprigs parsley

Add the seasonings (little salt because the chicken broth is salted). Check later and add more if needed.

Tie the thyme, bay leaf, parsley (a bouquet garni) in a cheesecloth bag and press deep into the middle of the stew. They can be put in without the cheesecloth, but since the stew should be creamy and smooth, the herbs should be removed before serving, and the cheesecloth makes it easier. Bring to a simmer. Cover and simmer 15 minutes on very low flame.

ADDED VEGETABLES
½ pound button mush-
   rooms, or more
Boiling water
1 tablespoon butter
2 teaspoons lemon juice

Blanch the mushrooms by cooking them in boiling water to cover, with butter and lemon juice for 5 minutes. (If large mushrooms are used, cut in ¼-inch slices.) Drain and add to the stew. The mushrooms can be prepared beforehand and set aside.

Bring stew to a simmer again, cover and cook 15 minutes more, or until chicken is tender. Tip pot and skim off fat. Check and correct seasoning. Remove cheesecloth bag and turn stew into a clean warm flameproof casserole.

For later serving, allow the stew to cool with lid askew before refrigerating. To reheat, bring very slowly to a simmer. Simmer just long enough to heat through.

TO FINISH
1 cup heavy cream
2 egg yolks, beaten
Juice of ½ lemon

Add half the cream, bring back to a simmer. Mix egg yolks with the rest of the cream and the lemon juice. Stir into the stew. Heat but do not allow to boil.

GARNISHES
4 tablespoons finely
   chopped parsley
1 pimiento, cut up

Garnish with parsley and pimiento.

Brunswick Stew

for 6   about 2½ hours to cook

Succotash—a stew of corn and beans—came to the colonists from the Indians. The Pilgrims added meat, and when the dish moved south to the Virginias and Carolinas, it took the name of the county that popularized it. Brunswick was originally made with squirrel. Today chicken replaces it; but many Seaboarders insist on rabbit, Piedmonters on wild

cook in:

5-6 qt.

serve in bowls,
from a 4 qt. casserole

or a tureen

MEATS
1 ham hock (about ½
pound)
1 three-inch piece of veal
shank
Giblets and neck of 3–4-
pound chicken
1 three- to four-pound
roasting chicken, cut up

LIQUIDS
1 can chicken broth
(about 2 cups)
Water to cover

POT VEGETABLE
Tops from 3 stalks celery

fowl. In Kentucky it becomes Burgoo, and anything goes in, even okra. The corn and beans preserve their identity, and potato provides the thickening. The trick is not to overcook the chicken, which may simmer only 40 minutes or so in the rich stock of giblets, veal shank, and ham hock. It is a surprisingly easy stew to make, the meat being removed for dicing when done, to be added again when the stock is reduced to the desired thickness—about that of a heavy soup. It is wonderful warmed up, and some should be saved to serve with cold ham or steak.

Brunswick stew is a meal in itself, but you might serve oysters or clams as a first course, with a bottle of Chablis or Muscadet or California Pinot Chardonnay. If you eliminate a first course, cider, cold and hard, is good with the stew, and so is beer. Salad is redundant. Ice cream, green apple pie, or berry tarts make fine desserts. Calvados, in or with black coffee, glorifies the apple flavor.

Pour 2 quarts water into a 5- or 6-quart kettle and measure where it comes to in the pot. This is the amount of stock you need to end up with, and doing this now saves measuring later. Throw out the water and start the recipe.

Wash ham hock, veal shank, and chicken neck and giblets; place in the kettle. Reserve the chicken.

Add chicken broth and water to cover completely.

Add celery and seasonings.

SEASONINGS
2 teaspoons salt
1 teaspoon freshly ground
black pepper

Bring to a boil; reduce to a simmer; skim off scum as it appears. Simmer 1½ hours or until ham and veal are almost coming off the bones. Add water during cooking just to keep everything covered.

Add chicken pieces; bring back to a simmer; skim.

Simmer 30 minutes or until chicken is ready to come off bones. Drain; reserve stock. Pick out the hock, shank, and chicken; remove skin and bones; leave meats in large bite-size pieces. Strain stock; skim off fat. Turn up heat and boil vigorously if necessary to reduce stock to 2 quarts (see beginning of recipe). Put all the meats in the stock.

ADDED VEGETABLES
2 medium onions, chopped
4 medium potatoes in
1-inch dice
1 one-pound-thirteen-
ounce can tomatoes,
drained
1 package frozen baby
lima beans
1 package frozen whole-
kernel corn

Add the onions, potatoes, and tomatoes. Bring to a simmer and cook 20 minutes.

Add the frozen lima beans; bring to a simmer; cook 10 minutes. Add frozen corn; cook until lima beans are tender, about 10 minutes more. Stir occasionally during addition of vegetables to prevent sticking.

ADDED SEASONINGS
¼ teaspoon crushed red
pepper
1 tablespoon Worcester-
shire sauce
¼ cup Fino Sherry

Stir in red pepper (use less or more, as desired), Worcestershire sauce, and Sherry. Check seasoning, adjust to taste. Keep stirring over very low heat until stew is a glorious mush, about 5 minutes.

Turn into a 4-quart casserole or tureen for serving.

For later serving, cool and refrigerate. To reheat, remove any hardened fat, cover, and place in a preheated 325° oven for 30–45 minutes or until stew is just warmed through.

Fish and Seafood

Äigo-Sau

cook in:

3 qt.

serve in bowls,

with sauce

FISH
2 pounds fresh white-fleshed fish fillets, in 2-inch pieces

This dish from Provence is a rich fish stew with potatoes. Different kinds of white-fleshed fish are used, the more the merrier. The fish, potatoes and onions, tomatoes and garlic are cooked in water and seasoned with fennel, orange peel, bay leaf, parsley, and celery. A rouille sauce of garlic and hot peppers served with it is used much the way the pistou is in Pistou Soup: it is so hot, though, it is served on the side. The soup can be served in bowls, separately, followed by the fish and vegetables; or you can serve everything together in large soup plates.

A Provençal wine—white, red, or rosé—will suit the dish and a first course of salami or Oeufs Durs Mayonnaise.* Follow the stew with salad and a goat or blue cheese—the only ones which will be noticed after the rouille. Dessert should be light and cooling, perhaps just fresh fruit and coffee.

Buy a variety of fish, but try to find types that cook in the same amount of time. The fish dealer can help you. Cut in uniform serving-size pieces.

VEGETABLES
5 or 6 medium potatoes,
  peeled, in ¼-inch slices
2 large tomatoes, peeled
  and chopped
1 medium onion, in thin
  rings
2 cloves garlic, minced

SEASONINGS
1 teaspoon salt
¼ teaspoon freshly ground
  black pepper
1 bay leaf
1 celery stalk, broken into
  two pieces
2 sprigs parsley
⅛ teaspoon fennel seeds
2 three-inch strips orange
  peel

FAT
⅓ cup olive oil

LIQUID
Boiling water

Arrange the fish in the bottom of a 3-quart shallow flame-proof casserole (preferably enameled ironware). Cover the fish with the potatoes. Put the tomatoes, onion, and garlic on top of the potatoes.

Sprinkle with salt and pepper.

Add the rest of the seasonings. Instead of the fennel seeds, 1 tablespoon Pec, Pernod, or other licorice-tasting spirit can be added at the end.

Pour in the olive oil.

Cover everything with boiling water. Bring to a boil; simmer gently for 20 minutes, or until potatoes are tender.

Check and correct seasoning. Remove bay leaf, celery, parsley, and orange peel.

ROUILLE SAUCE
2 garlic cloves
2 hot red peppers, or
  1 teaspoon dried red
  pepper
3 tablespoons fine bread
  crumbs
3 tablespoons olive oil
1 cup broth from the stew

GARNISH
¼ cup finely chopped fresh
  parsley

Pound the garlic and red peppers in a mortar, or chop extremely fine. Add the bread crumbs, then the olive oil, little by little, to incorporate it well, until you have a paste. Gradually add the broth, mix well, and put in a small bowl for serving.

As with most fish soup-stews, this is best made to serve immediately. If it has to be reheated, bring it very slowly to a simmer, just to heat through. Do not cook further.

Sprinkle with parsley.

Bouillabaisse

cook in:

5 qt.

serve in bowls, from
the pot or a tureen

for 6–8   about 20 minutes to cook

The excellence of this saffrony fish stew of Marseilles depends on the careful addition of the fish at different times, so they finish cooking at the same time. The broth is a stout balance of saffron with fennel, rosemary, orange rind, a bouquet garni, onions, garlic, tomatoes, and leeks if possible. Despite the fuss, this is a casual dish and many a shore cook here has produced a wonder. Ardent epicures insist that the secret is to have six fish, always including *rascasse,* which unites and brings out the flavors of the other fish, but the argument is empty because *rascasse* isn't available here. The superb flavor probably comes from cooking firm-fleshed and softer fish together. Other fierce adherents insist on having mussels or clams but no lobster or crab, and there are those who believe the reverse, but both schools are scorned by purists who say no shellfish at all. Along the Mediterranean the dish varies endlessly. Our recipe omits the controversial lobster and crab, but by all means use them if you wish. Buy them live if you can, split them, and add them with the firm-fleshed fish. Any dry white wine, young and fresh, is fine. Plenty of good crusty bread, a salad, and fresh fruit complete the meal. Beforehand you might serve pastis, which is Pec, Pernod, or Ricard with ice and water, with Antipasto* for the starving.

At the fish store pick out fish from the 2 categories, preferably 6 different kinds. Have the fish dealer prepare the fish in uniform chunks, large bite-size pieces, and save all trimmings for stock. If you use eel, have it peeled.

Keep the firm fish separate from the soft. They are cooked at different times. To make stock: boil fish heads, bones, and trimmings in 2½ quarts water and 2 teaspoons salt for 30 minutes; strain, pressing out juices. Set aside to use later.

Wash and scrub clams well until washing water is clean and clear. Shell and devein shrimp. Set aside.

Heat the olive oil in a high, narrow, lidded kettle or deep, lidded flameproof 5- or 6-quart casserole.

Slowly cook the onions, garlic, and leeks until tender, but not brown. Add the tomatoes and cook briefly together.

FISH
3–4 pounds fish fillets, ½ firm-fleshed (eel, cod, haddock, halibut, sea bass), ½ soft-fleshed (sole, red snapper, flounder, sea perch, hake, mullet, whiting)

SHELLFISH
3 dozen clams
1 pound raw shrimp

FAT
⅓ cup olive oil

POT VEGETABLES
2 large onions, chopped
3 garlic cloves, chopped
3 leeks, white part only, chopped, about ¾ inch in diameter (optional)
3 large ripe tomatoes, peeled, seeded, and chopped

SEASONINGS
- ½ teaspoon thyme
- 1 bay leaf
- 2 tablespoons finely chopped fresh parsley
- ¼ teaspoon rosemary
- ¼ teaspoon fennel seeds
- 1 teaspoon grated orange rind

Stir in the seasonings. (One or 2 tablespoons of a licorice-flavored liqueur—Pec, Pernod, Ricard, or Ojen—can be substituted for the fennel. Add it after the saffron.) Lay the firm fish pieces on top of the vegetable mixture. Simmer 5 minutes. Add the soft fish.

LIQUID
- Fish stock, or 1½ quarts water and 1 quart bottled clam juice

Add either the home-made stock or the water and clam juice.

ADDITIONAL SEASONINGS
- 1 teaspoon saffron threads
- ¼ teaspoon freshly ground black pepper
- ⅛ teaspoon cayenne pepper

Add saffron, rubbing between thumb and forefinger to break up the threads; add pepper and cayenne. Taste for salt, but remember that both stock and clam juice are salty. Simmer 5 minutes.

Add clams and shrimp. Cover and cook just until clams open, 5–10 minutes.

GARNISH
- ¼ cup finely chopped fresh parsley

Sprinkle with parsley.

This dish does not reheat, but much of it can be done ahead. Refrigerate the fish in 3 separate containers: firm, soft, and shellfish. Make the stock, cook the vegetables, and add the seasonings. Thirty minutes before serving time, proceed with the recipe.

New England Clam Chowder

cook in:

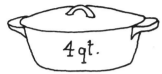

4 qt.

serve in bowls

New England Clam Chowder is one of America's greatest dishes. For 2 dozen chowder clams you want about 6 cups liquid. When the clams are steamed with a dry white wine, they produce about 4 cups broth, so cream is added to make up the difference. If you buy clams already shucked (2 dozen clams are about a pint) make up the liquid with 2 cups milk and 2 cups cream. If you must use canned clams, measure the liquid and add enough water or white wine to make 2 cups, then add 2 cups cream and 2 cups milk.

Clam chowder is a rich and fortifying dish, but something more seems called for. To make a meal of it, serve a large salad, followed by a goodly selection of cheeses and of course good French or Italian bread. Any dry white wine suits the chowder—particularly a Chablis or Muscadet or California Chardonnay—but a light Pilsener beer is good, too. Apple pie is a satisfying dessert, with Calvados and coffee.

CLAMS
    2 dozen chowder clams
    Dry white wine (Muscadet or California Pinot Blanc), or water, or dry Vermouth

Make sure all clams are tightly shut when you buy them. Scrub them thoroughly, and place them in a 4-quart heavy, lidded flameproof casserole. Pour in the wine (or water or dry Vermouth) to the depth of ½ inch. Cover and cook on a medium flame 10–15 minutes or until all clams are open. If one or two have not opened, discard them. Strain and reserve liquid. If it is less than 4 cups, add water to make 4 cups. Shuck clams. Mince the hard parts, which will be obvious to the touch. Leave the rest whole. Wash and dry the pot.

FAT
    ¼ pound salt pork in ¼-inch dice, or ¼ pound bacon in ¼-inch dice

In the casserole, slowly cook the salt pork or bacon until fat is rendered and bacon or pork is crisp. With a slotted spoon remove it to a paper towel for draining. Pour off all but 2 tablespoons of the fat.

POT VEGETABLES
1 medium onion, finely
chopped
3 medium potatoes, in ½-
inch dice

Slowly cook the onion in the bacon fat until limp but not brown. Add the potatoes and the minced hard parts of the clams.

SEASONINGS
¼ teaspoon white pepper
Pinch of thyme
Dash of Tabasco
(optional)

Add the seasonings. No salt is specified because the clam liquid is salty, but check after adding cream, and add some to taste if necessary.

LIQUIDS
4 cups clam liquid, or mixture of clam liquid and
water
2 cups heavy cream or
half and half, heated
1–2 tablespoons Cognac
(optional)

Add the clam liquid or mixture of clam juice and water and cook gently until the potatoes are tender, about 10–15 minutes.

Add the hot cream, the salt pork or bacon bits and the soft parts of the clams. Cook just to warm the clams. Add the Cognac, if used.

GARNISH
Paprika

Sprinkle with paprika.

Manhattan Clam Chowder

for 6   about 45 minutes to cook

cook in:

4 qt.

Manhattan puts tomatoes in clam chowder, although it is considered a crime east of the Connecticut River. The dish came originally from the Atlantic coast of France, where a *chaudière* is the pot a *chaudrée* is cooked in, a seaside stew made of whatever is available. The dish came south from Quebec to the Dutch colony of New Amsterdam, where the tomatoes crept in. Similar dishes are made wherever shell-

serve in bowls,
from a 4 qt. casserole

or from a tureen

CLAMS

2 dozen chowder clams
Dry white wine (Musca-
det or California Pinot
Blanc), or dry Ver-
mouth, or water

FAT

¼ pound salt pork, or ¼
pound thickly sliced
bacon, diced in ¼-inch
pieces

fish is at hand. This version includes the best of several worlds.

There is no first course for Manhattan Clam Chowder, except perhaps corn on the cob, preferably roasted in the husk. Nothing really goes with it except lots of bread and plenty of beer, or some more of the Muscadet or California Pinot Blanc you have used for the stewing. Nothing follows it, except a second helping, or some cheese and more beer or wine. It is not a dish to taste simply out of curiosity, for it can become an addiction, even a way of life. This recipe should really be recommended only to those people who live on or near a seacoast, for it is not the same when the clams are canned.

Make sure all the clams are tightly shut when you buy them. Scrub them well and place in a pot or kettle with a well-fitting lid. Pour ½ inch dry white wine (or dry Vermouth or water) in the bottom of the kettle. Put in the clams, cover and cook on medium heat about 10 minutes or until all clams are open. If 1 or 2 have not opened, discard them.

Strain and reserve liquid; shuck clams. Mince hard parts; they will be obvious to the touch. Leave the rest whole.

In a heavy, lidded nonmetallic (preferably enameled ironware) pot, 4- or 4½-quart, slowly cook the salt pork or bacon until it renders its fat and is golden brown.

VEGETABLES
2 medium onions, chopped
1 medium green pepper, chopped
2 stalks celery, chopped
2 leeks, white part only, finely chopped (optional)
2 medium carrots in ¼-inch dice
3 medium potatoes in ¾-inch dice
1-pound-3-ounce can tomatoes (about 3 cups)

Add the onions, green pepper, celery, and leeks (if used). Cook slowly, stirring, until they are tender but not brown. Add the carrots and potatoes. Stir and cook gently together for 5 minutes.

Add the tomatoes.

SEASONINGS
½ teaspoon pepper
½ teaspoon thyme
1 bay leaf
2 tablespoons finely chopped fresh parsley

Add the seasonings. Bring to a simmer. Cover and cook on a very low flame for 20 minutes, or until vegetables are almost tender.

LIQUIDS
Clam liquid
Water

Measure liquid from clams. If it is less than 4 cups, add water to bring it to 4 cups. Add to the pot. Add the minced hard parts of clams. Simmer, covered, 15–20 minutes, or until vegetables are tender. Add the rest of the clams; cook just to heat through—about 2 minutes. Check for salt.

This stew can be reheated but it would be better to do in advance all the vegetable part, and complete with the clams just before serving.

GARNISH
¼ cup finely chopped fresh parsley

Sprinkle with parsley.

Creole Jambalaya

cook in:

3-4 qt.

serve in same, or:

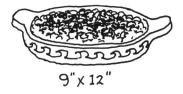

9" x 12"

MEAT
  1 pound ham in 1-inch
    cubes

FATS
  1 tablespoon butter
  1 tablespoon ham fat

POT VEGETABLES
  1 large green pepper,
    chopped
  1 large onion, chopped
  4 medium tomatoes,
    peeled and chopped, or 3
    cups canned tomatoes,
    chopped

When Africans were introduced to the French kitchens of New Orleans, a miracle happened that came to be called Creole cooking. From *jambon,* the French for ham, they evolved the word *jambalaya,* giving it an added upbeat, and this zest is the spirit of Creole cooking, the jazz of cuisine. When in doubt, the French add a bouquet garni, but a Creole tosses in a red pepper or whatever to spice the dish, and usually something more. In this case, it is shrimp.

A multitude of drinks taste good with jambalaya—Pimm's Cup, beer, even tea, either iced or hot—but a soft white wine may be best of all, a Meursault, a Graves, a Soave, or a Gray Riesling from California. The dish is filling, so a light first course of crackers and Münster or Gouda is enough. A generous salad with avocado and a dressing with a little lime in it is delicious. Dessert might be a custard or a chocolate mousse, followed by Café Royale—black coffee which you set aflame by putting a sugar cube in a spoonful of Cognac, lighting it and sliding it onto the surface of the coffee.

Trim fat from ham. Reserve and chop 1 tablespoon of the fat.

In a 3- or 4-quart flameproof casserole (preferably enameled ironware) cook the ham fat briefly in the butter. Discard the ham fat, and lightly cook the ham in the butter.

Add green pepper and onion, and slowly cook until they are tender but not brown. Add tomatoes.

THICKENING
1 tablespoon flour
1 tablespoon soft butter

Mix together, with fork or fingers, the flour and butter. Stir into vegetable and ham mixture.

LIQUID
2 cups boiling water, more if needed during cooking

Add water.

SEASONINGS
1 clove garlic, minced
¼ cup finely chopped fresh parsley
½ teaspoon thyme
1 tablespoon Worcestershire sauce
¼ teaspoon cayenne or ½ teaspoon dried red peppers or ⅛ teaspoon Tabasco
1 teaspoon salt

Add seasonings.

Bring to a boil.

RICE
1½ cups long-grained rice

Stir in rice; bring to a simmer.

SHRIMP
2 pounds raw shrimp, shelled and deveined

Add shrimp, cover and simmer, stirring occasionally, for 30 minutes or until rice is cooked and liquid absorbed. The jambalaya should be moist. If it gets too dry during cooking add a little boiling water.

This dish is better made at the time of serving, but it can be made ahead up to the point of adding rice and shrimp.

GARNISH
¼ cup finely chopped fresh parsley

Sprinkle with parsley.

Solianka

cook in:

3 qt.

serve in bowls, from the pot

This remarkable stew demonstrates the masterful Russian way with salmon. It is cooked in a simple homemade fish stock with onions and tomatoes and has the added fillip of dill pickles, olives, and capers. The taste is unexpectedly subtle and indefinable, and it looks beautiful—pink salmon in a broth colored faintly by the tomatoes, garnished with green and black olives and lemon slices. Serve it with Crisp Garlic Bread.*

Herring and drafts of icy vodka would taste good before the Solianka and cucumbers with dill are a nice accompaniment. A baked Alaska would be a marvelous dessert, but that's ridiculous. A simpler one would be vanilla ice cream with brandied peaches.

FISH STOCK
  2 pounds fish bones and
     heads
  2 quarts water
  1 teaspoon salt
  ¼ teaspoon white pepper

Ask your fish dealer to save some fish trimmings. Put them in a saucepan with 2 quarts water. Bring to a boil, and boil gently for 30 minutes. Strain and reserve stock.

FAT
  2 tablespoons olive oil

Put the oil in a 3-quart shallow flameproof casserole.

POT VEGETABLES

3 large tomatoes, peeled, seeded, chopped, or 2 one-pound cans tomatoes, well drained

2 medium onions, finely chopped

4 small or 2 large dill pickles, finely chopped

1 teaspoon chopped pitted green olives

1 teaspoon chopped pitted black olives

1 teaspoon capers

Add the tomatoes and cook slowly, stirring until they form a paste. Add the onions. Add the dill pickles, olives, and capers to the other vegetables, stirring to mix.

FISH

1½ pounds salmon, cut in 2-inch strips

Add the salmon.

LIQUID

Fish stock

Add the fish stock.

SEASONINGS

1 bay leaf
2 parsley sprigs
Salt and pepper

Add the bay leaf and parsley. Check seasoning and add salt and pepper to taste. Bring to a simmer, and simmer 10 minutes.

TO FINISH (optional)

4 tablespoons butter

Stir in the butter. This is for enrichment and can be omitted.

Like most fish stews, this is better served fresh, but it is still good warmed up. The whole sauce can be made ahead, up to the point of adding salmon. To reheat, bring slowly to a simmer, heat through, but do not cook further. Remove parsley and bay leaf before serving.

    4 green olives, pitted
    4 black olives, pitted
    Thin lemon slices

Seafare Stew

cook in:

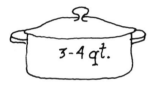

3-4 qt.

serve in same

STOCK
    1–2 pounds fish heads and
        scraps
    2 quarts unsalted water

FISH
    ½ pound fresh bay scal-
        lops or quartered sea
        scallops
    ½ pound raw shrimp,
        shelled and deveined
    1 pound fillet of haddock
        in 2-inch squares
    12 small clams

Garnish with sliced olives and lemon slices. Serve in bowls or soup plates.

for 4   40 minutes–1 hour for stock to cook
              about 30 minutes for the stew

Fish cooks in no time at all, but a good stock is needed to produce an appropriately rich sauce and the simmering takes a while. This sauce can be made ahead so that the cook can produce a masterly dish while the guests have a drink. The trace of licorice from the anise-flavored liqueur unites flavors and adds subtlety to the stew's aroma. Crusty bread, plain or with garlic,* goes with it.

A white wine of Provence or Italy—Cassis or Bandol, Soave or Orvieto—suits the Mediterranean character of this dish. Crisp raw vegetables with a Sour Cream and Dill or Green Sauce* could either precede the stew or replace a salad. Salty cheeses like Greek Feta or a selection of goat cheeses could follow, with fresh fruit for dessert.

Wash the fish heads and scraps thoroughly. Place in a saucepan with water and simmer gently 40–60 minutes, or until liquid has cooked down to one-half. Strain stock, discarding solids. If there is less than 1 quart liquid, add water to make 4 cups and reserve.

Wash fish and seafood; scrub the clams.

FAT
2 tablespoons olive oil

In a 3½- or 4-quart lidded flameproof casserole, heat the oil and lightly cook the shallots and green pepper until they are tender but not brown. Stir in the garlic.

POT VEGETABLES
¼ cup chopped shallots, or
¼ cup chopped white of
scallions and a small
garlic clove, minced
1 green pepper in strips
2 garlic cloves, minced

LIQUIDS
2 cups tomato purée
1 cup dry white wine, like
Soave or Orvieto
4 cups fish stock

Add the liquids.

SEASONINGS
¼ cup finely chopped fresh
parsley
⅛ teaspoon crushed red
pepper
1 teaspoon saffron
threads, crushed
½ teaspoon dried basil
2 teaspoons salt
½ teaspoon freshly ground
black pepper

Add the seasonings, bring to a simmer, partially cover, and simmer 15 minutes. Check the seasoning; add up to 1 teaspoon more salt to taste. For more hotness, add more red pepper, or a pinch of cayenne or a dash of Tobasco.

Add the scallops, shrimp, and haddock; simmer uncovered 10 minutes. Add the clams, cover, and simmer until clams open—about 5 minutes. Serve immediately in large soup plates or bowls.

This stew can be made ahead up to the point of adding the fish and seafood.

TO FINISH
2 tablespoons Pernod,
Ricard, or Pec

Just before serving, stir in liqueur.

GARNISH
1 four-ounce can or jar
pimientos, chopped

Sprinkle pimientos over the stew.

Tripe

Portuguese Tripe

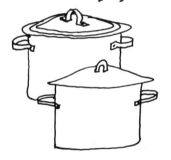

cook in large pots

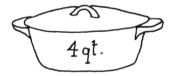

assemble in:

4 qt.

Americans do not like tripe, and it's a pity because there are many wonderful stews made of it. Tripe is the classic dish of Oporto, whose citizens are called *tripeiros*. Tripe recipes are extraordinarily long, and so is the cooking time.

In this stew the various elements are cooked separately, then assembled. It is a lot of work but worth it. The actual cooking time is hard to calculate because things are done separately. The beans, for instance, soak for an hour and cook for an hour and a half. The tripe has to be blanched and then cooked for at least three hours. The chicken, ham, and chorizo cook for the better part of an hour. Then, after the onions are cooked in oil and the whole thing is assembled, it cooks another couple of hours. It is a good dish to do ahead because it is improved by a day in the refrigerator, and except for rice, good bread, and a melon for dessert, your dinner is all in the pot, ready to be heated and served. Have lots of rough red wine to drink with the meal and a bottle of old Port with the melon.

BEANS
   1 cup dried white beans
   (Great Northern, navy,
   or baby lima)

Rinse beans, and place in a saucepan with 6 cups water. Bring to a boil; boil 2 minutes. Remove from heat, and allow to stand for 1 hour. Bring to a boil again, add 1 teaspoon salt, and simmer 1½ hours or until beans are just tender. Allow them to stand in liquid until called for in recipe.

TRIPE
   2 pounds honeycomb tripe
   in ½-by-2-inch strips

The tripe is cooked separately and finished in stock with other ingredients. Wash it thoroughly in cold water. Place in a large lidded pot or kettle. Cover with clean cold water, and bring to a boil. Boil 5 minutes, drain, and rinse with cold water.

POT VEGETABLE
   Tops from 1 bunch celery

Place tripe again in the kettle with the celery tops.

SEASONING
   1 tablespoon salt

Add salt.

LIQUIDS
   3 quarts cold water
   2 tablespoons cider vinegar

Add water and vinegar, bring to a boil, cover partially and simmer 3–4 hours, the longer the better. Replace water as it boils away.

While tripe is cooking make stock.

2 pounds veal bones
1 ham hock (about ½ pound)
3 celery stalks, broken in half
2 carrots, halved lengthwise
2 medium onions, quartered
2 cloves garlic, mashed
3 sprigs parsley
1 tablespoon salt
¼ teaspoon pepper
3–4 quarts water, or enough to cover

FAT
2 tablespoons olive oil

ADDED VEGETABLES
2 medium onions, finely chopped
6 medium carrots in ½-inch slices
3 cups canned tomatoes

ADDED MEAT
½ pound chorizo (Spanish sausage) in ¼-inch slices (See p. 232 for sources.)

Wash veal bones, hock, and vegetables. There is no need to peel garlic or carrots, since they will be strained out. Place in another lidded pot or kettle. Bring to a boil, boil gently 10–15 minutes, skimming off scum as it appears. When scum stops appearing, add salt and pepper. Partially cover and simmer very slowly 2 hours. Replace water during cooking just to keep everything covered. Skim occasionally.

Remove ham hocks, cool, peel, remove ham from bones, chop against the grain, and reserve. Continue cooking the rest for 1 hour more. Drain tripe, discard celery, discard liquid, reserve tripe.

Turn on oven to 300°.

In a 4-quart lidded flameproof casserole, in which you will serve the dish, heat the oil; cook the onions until they are limp and transparent, but not brown. Add the carrots. Drain the tomatoes; chop fine (or blend in an electric blender). Add tomatoes and cook very slowly for about 10 minutes or until the mixture is no longer watery.

Add the chorizo.

Parboiled white beans
Tripe
Ham
Veal stock

Drain the beans; add with the tripe and ham to the casserole. Add about 2 cups veal stock or enough to not quite cover the contents of the casserole. Stir gently to mix. Place in the preheated 300° oven, and cook, covered, for 1 hour. Then remove lid and cook, stirring occasionally, for another hour. If it gets too dry, add just enough stock to prevent sticking or burning. The stew is supposed to be thick and moist.

Turn off oven; place a clean dish towel over the casserole and replace the lid. Let stand ½–¾ hour in the oven. The towel absorbs the steam and makes the stew drier. For later serving, cool and refrigerate. To reheat, bring to room temperature; place in a preheated 325° oven for 30–45 minutes or until stew is just warmed through. Test with fingers.

Note: Canned white beans can be used, but they will not hold up very well over the long cooking in the oven. If used they should be drained, washed, and carefully stirred in just before the oven is turned off.

Leftover stock can be frozen and saved for later use.

GARNISH
¼ cup finely chopped fresh
parsley

Sprinkle with parsley.

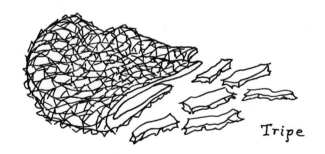

Tripe

Oxtails

Oxtail Ragoût

cook in:

5-6 qt

serve in same, or
9"x 12" baking dish

MEAT
4 pounds oxtails (3 or 4
pieces per person)

LIQUIDS
Water to cover (about 8–
10 cups)
2 cups tomato purée (1
one-pound can)

POT VEGETABLE
4 medium onions, coarsely
sliced

Out of Central Europe, by way of Canada, comes this simple boiled stew of oxtails with vegetables. It is made like the basic unbrowned beef stew except for the tomatoes in the sauce, but oxtails have a special flavor of their own. A full-bodied wine of the Rhône or Italy tastes good with it, and it could be preceded by a flowery Riesling with a first course of Cold Shrimp* or smoked salmon with cucumbers and Sour Cream and Dill Sauce.* A salad with endive or chicory would add a nice contrast, paving the way for a rich Viennese torte.

Wash and drain the oxtail pieces. Place in a large uncovered pot on the top of the stove.

Cover with water and bring to an easy boil. Skim off the scum as it appears on the surface. Boil 15–20 minutes or until no more scum appears. Add tomato purée.

Add the onions. Bring to a simmer.

SEASONINGS
- 2 teaspoons salt
- ¼ teaspoon freshly ground black pepper
- 1 bay leaf
- 1 tablespoon Worcestershire sauce

Add the seasonings; continue to simmer, skimming off any fat as it accumulates on the top. Cook partially covered for about 2 hours or until the meat is nearly coming off the bones, but not quite.

ADDED VEGETABLES
- 2 cups coarsely sliced celery
- 1 cup coarsely chopped green pepper
- 6 medium potatoes, halved
- 6 carrots in 2-inch pieces, thick ends halved to make uniform-sized pieces

Add the vegetables and continue cooking for ½–¾ hour or until the vegetables are tender.

Remove the solids to a clean lidded casserole or pile up in a shallow baking dish that can be brought to the table. Skim fat from the liquid in the cooking pot and check seasoning.

THICKENING
- 2 tablespoons flour mixed with 4 tablespoons cold water, or 1 tablespoon cornstarch mixed with 2 tablespoons cold water

Stir the flour and water or cornstarch and water mixture into the stew liquid in the pot. (Cornstarch makes a more transparent thickening.) Cook 5 minutes more.

For a thicker gravy, add more flour or cornstarch in small amounts, always well mixed with cold water, until desired thickness is reached. Pour the liquid over the stew in the casserole or baking dish. The sauce should not completely cover everything. If there is any left over, serve it in a bowl on the side, or keep it for soup at another time. Cover the casserole with its lid, or cover the baking dish well with foil.

To serve immediately, place in 350° oven for 10–15 minutes to heat thoroughly.

For later serving, leave the stew in the cooking vessel; cool, partially covered. When it is thoroughly cool, cover and refrigerate. To reheat, remove the hardened fat from the top of the stew; bring slowly to a simmer on top of the stove. Turn into a warm casserole or warm baking dish, reserving any excess of liquid, as above.

TO FINISH
½ cup finely chopped fresh
    parsley

Sprinkle with parsley.

Vegetables

Soupe au Pistou

cook in:

5-6 qt.

serve in a tureen

VEGETABLES
2 cups carrots in ½-inch
  dice
2 cups potatoes in ¾-inch
  dice
2 cups chopped onion or
  2 cups sliced leeks

for 6–8   about 1 hour to cook

Pistou is the French Riviera's version of Italian minestrone and Genoese Il Pesto, a soup-stew that is named for its sauce of fresh sweet basil and garlic, oil and Gruyère-like cheese, mashed together. Such cheese doesn't mash easily, so grated Parmesan is substituted here. Our Parisian relatives add tomato purée but that is frowned on in Nice, where Pistou is a specialty. The fresh sweet basil gives the Pistou its distinction, but it is worth making with dried basil. The sauce can be made by itself and used for spaghetti, fish, or veal. As for the soup, the more vegetables the better, particularly any fresh white beans you can find.

This is a marvelous dish to top off a cold buffet or an Antipasto* and is splendid before a grilled fish or steak. Any simple table wine is fine with Pistou, and so is beer.

The root vegetables go in first because they take longest to cook. If leeks are available, use leeks, white part only, instead of onion. New potatoes are best; regular boiling potatoes will do, but baking potatoes will not. Other root vegetables, such as white or yellow turnips or parsnips, can be substituted or added.

LIQUIDS
8 cups canned chicken broth
4 cups water
1 cup tomato purée

SEASONINGS
1 teaspoon salt
¼ teaspoon freshly ground black pepper

ADDITIONAL VEGETABLES AND PASTA
2 cups fresh green beans in ½-inch pieces or 1 package frozen cut beans
½ cup vermicelli broken into 2-inch pieces
2 cups canned kidney beans

ADDITIONAL SEASONING
½ teaspoon crumbled saffron threads

PISTOU SAUCE
4 garlic cloves minced
¼ cup chopped fresh basil or 1 tablespoon dried basil
¼ to ½ cup olive oil
6 tablespoons grated Parmesan cheese

Place the vegetables in a 6-quart kettle with the liquids. The liquid can also be all water (3 quarts, 1 tablespoon salt).

Add the salt and pepper; bring to a boil. Boil gently for 40 minutes.

Add the green beans and vermicelli; cook 20 minutes. Add kidney beans; cook 5 minutes.

Stir in the saffron.

Place all the ingredients for the pistou in a blender. Blend to the consistency of mayonnaise, using more oil if necessary. To do by hand, mash together the garlic and basil, add oil and cheese in small amounts, beating to a smooth paste. Put the pistou in the bottom of a soup tureen or 4-quart casserole. Stir in 1 cup soup; gradually add the rest of the soup, stirring to blend. Sprinkle with lots of parsley.

Before, During,
and After the Stew

SOME ADDITIONAL RECIPES

FIRST COURSES

A first course is not essential, and if one is served, it should be light, only whetting the appetite for what is to come. Some of the following may be served with drinks, as a change from the usual cocktail snacks. Most of them may be prepared ahead and eaten while the stew finishes its cooking, or while it is being reheated.

Raw Vegetable Combinations

Raw vegetables are delicious with drinks and as a first course; this list of combinations may suggest others. The vegetables should be prepared well ahead of time so that they can be allowed to stand in ice water for at least an hour before serving. A few ice cubes on or among them when they are served helps keep them crisp and cold. They are good with nothing but salt. Green Sauce,* Sour Cream and Dill Sauce,* or Mayonnaise Sauce* is also good as a dip.

—Endive, sliced lengthwise, watercress and black olives
—Small flowerets of cauliflower with cherry tomatoes and green pepper strips
—Flowerets of broccoli and cauliflower, with radishes
—Radishes alone, with the root cut off and 2 inches of the green top trimmed and left on, served with sweet butter and French bread
—Cherry tomatoes and lots of watercress
—Slivers of carrot and celery with black olives and watercress

—Celery cut in 3-inch pieces, with lengthwise cuts at each end and almost to the center, allowed to stand in ice water for an hour or two until the ends curl, with green-pepper strips and radishes
—Matchsticks of white turnip, stuck into shaved ice, with tiny Greek or Italian ripe olives
—Fennel in lengthwise wedges, with sweet red-pepper strips, black olives, and watercress
—Cucumbers, peeled, halved, seeded, and then cut in strips; with tiny scallions, green and all; carrot strips; and broccoli flowerets
—Raw mushrooms sliced down through the stem, with olives and almonds.

Mock Soufflé on Toast

Something hot tastes good with drinks, and this is simple to make. It is equally good with both red and white wines.

6 slices toast, no crusts
¾ cup mayonnaise
2 tablespoons grated Parmesan cheese
1 small onion, finely chopped, or 2 tablespoons chopped chives
Freshly ground black pepper

Cool the toast on a rack so it will stay crisp. Cut each piece in 4. Mix together the mayonnaise, cheese, and onion or chives. Spread about a tablespoonful of the mixture on each quarter of toast; sprinkle with some more Parmesan and a grind of pepper. Place under the broiler, set at 325°, for 5–7 minutes, until just golden. Serves 4–6.

Hummus (Chick-pea spread)

Drain the chick peas through a sieve. Wash them thoroughly by running cold water over them until the water runs clear. Spread them out on paper towels and pat them dry.

2 cups (a 1-pound can) chick peas (garbanzos)
1 tablespoon onion, minced
2 garlic cloves, minced

Place the chick peas, onion, garlic, salt, cayenne, ½ cup of oil, and the lemon juice in the blender. Blend until you have a thick smooth purée, stopping the blender occasionally to

1 teaspoon salt
⅛ teaspoon cayenne
½–¾ cup vegetable oil or
  olive oil
Juice of 1 lemon (about ¼
  cup)
2 tablespoons chopped
  parsley
A few grinds of the pep-
  permill

stir and scrape down the sides. Add the rest of the oil, or even more if necessary to keep the blender from stalling. To do by hand, with a large spoon press the chick peas through a sieve, or put them through a food mill. Add the garlic, onion, salt, and cayenne. Beating constantly, add the oil little by little, to form a thick, smooth paste. Beat in the lemon juice.

Check for seasoning, adding more salt and lemon juice if desired. Sprinkle with parsley and pepper. Serve with warmed Syrian bread, if you can find it, or with sesame crackers. Makes 3 cups, enough for 6–8.

Other things to serve with drinks

Bread sticks are good with drinks, but somewhat bland. A spicier version may be made by wrapping one end of each bread stick with a paper-thin sliver of prosciutto. Stand the sticks in glasses, ham ends up. Most people will devour three or four apiece.

Dried beef, sometimes called chipped or spiced beef, is a tasty appetizer. Pull it apart into 2-inch pieces and serve it in the middle of a bowl of watercress, so the two can be eaten together, with the fingers; or serve on small plates. This could also be a first course, served with a Rhine wine. Or, if no cheese course is planned, the dried beef can be served with slivers of Feta cheese. About ¼ pound cheese and the same amount of dried beef, with a bunch of water-cress, serve 4.

A big bowl of nuts in their shells, plus a nutcracker, is an overlooked pleasure. Serve with drinks, they don't spoil the appetite for the stew to come, the way salted nuts do. Nuts are particularly good with Sherry, Vermouth, and the other fortified wines.

Hot Chicken Consommé

6 cups canned chicken
  broth, with fat removed
  from top
1 cup dry white wine
12 whole peppercorns
4 shallots, peeled and
  chopped
½ teaspoon thyme
1 small bay leaf
4 parsley sprigs
1 celery top

Hot broth is particularly appetizing and satisfactorily light before a hearty stew full of taste. Combine everything in a 3-quart saucepan, bring to a boil, and turn down to simmer for 30 minutes. Strain through a moistened and wrung-out kitchen towel. Taste, and add a little salt, if needed. Serve with a thin lemon slice and chopped parsley. Serves 4. For 6, add one more can of chicken broth, using the same amounts of the other ingredients.

Jellied Chicken Consommé

8 cups canned chicken
  broth, with fat removed
  from top
3 envelopes (3 ounces)
  unflavored gelatin
1 cup dry white wine
12 whole peppercorns
4 shallots, peeled and
  chopped
½ teaspoon thyme
1 small bay leaf
4 parsley sprigs
1 celery top
Salt to taste
2 tablespoons chopped
  chives
Lemon wedges

A cool course to serve before a rich or spicy stew. Moisten the gelatin with ¾ cup broth. Combine the rest of the broth with the rest of the ingredients in a 3-quart saucepan, bring to a boil, and turn down to simmer for 40 minutes. Check for salt, bearing in mind that cold dishes require more salt than hot ones. Strain broth into the moistened gelatin, stirring until gelatin is well dissolved. Cool, then chill for at least two hours, or until set. Chop the jellied consommé into cubes and serve in small bowls with chopped chives sprinkled over the top and a lemon wedge on the side. Serves 6.

Oeufs Durs Mayonnaise

Hard-boiled eggs with mayonnaise sounds more glamorous in French, and those who had to eat poor in Paris will never taste any without remembering Raffy's and the other student bistros around St. Germain des Prés. With wine and a ragoût, lunch was less than a dollar. Halved lengthwise and set on a lettuce leaf, the egg was crowned with a couple of tablespoons mayonnaise, sprinkled with capers and fresh black pepper and some parsley sprigs, usually two.

Unsweetened commercial mayonnaise can be adjusted for a creamier consistency and better taste by adding, for each ½ cup: 2 teaspoons olive oil and two teaspoons lemon juice, the oil added ½ teaspoon at a time, the lemon juice stirred in last. This will make four servings, but you might want another ½ cup in a bowl for those who want more. On this basis, 1 cup mayonnaise for 4, 1½ for 6, and so on.

Smoked Salmon

One of the nice things about good restaurants is the excellent Nova Scotia salmon they serve, with a wedge of lemon, some capers, and coarsely ground pepper, on lettuce with watercress or parsley. Few things taste better with a white wine before a veal or chicken stew. If the stew is not too rich the salmon tastes best with sour cream. At home, you can offer two or three slices instead of the slivers served in restaurants. A cup of Sour Cream and Dill Sauce* is more than enough for six, but any less looks skimpy.

Or mix cucumbers with the Sour Cream and Dill Sauce, and serve along with slices of the salmon. Two cucumbers with 1 cup of the sauce serves 4–6.

Antipasto

The idea of serving antipasto before a stew sounds marvelous, but when you're standing at the counter or drawing up a shopping list, it's hard to recall all the things that ought to go on a tray. To jog the memory, here's a list of items. Any six will make a delectable selection.

—Pimiento halves with an anchovy fillet on top
—Black and green olives
—Thinly sliced Genoa salami and sliced pepperoni sausage
—Canned artichoke hearts, drained and marinated in French dressing
—Whole button mushrooms or coarsely sliced larger ones, marinated in French dressing
—Canned pickled beets
—Cheese, preferably Provolone
—Hard-boiled eggs
—Thin strips of green and sweet red peppers
—Hot chili pickles
—Small scallions, green tops and all
—Wedges of tomato or cherry tomatoes
—Fennel
—Radishes
—Celery

Hors d'Oeuvre Varié

The French appetizer tray is more involved than antipasto. It is usually served in little matching oval or rectangular dishes, with a can of Portuguese sardines on a saucer, or a can of tuna fish, or some caviar or roe. The labels are decorative and make for visual variety. There is no reason at all, of course, why anything from the antipasto list should not be on the hors d'oeuvre tray. French bread and sweet butter are the customary accompaniments.

—Marinated mushrooms with minced chives and parsley
—Julienne of pickled beets
—Hard-boiled eggs with anchovy strips, or deviled eggs
—Fresh poached salmon with mayonnaise
—Italian or Greek olives, small and large
—Cooked Polish sausage (kielbasa) or salami, thinly sliced
—Cold small shrimp with dill
—Herring, pickled in white wine
—Radishes

—In Sauce Vinaigrette* in separate dishes:
    Sliced tomatoes
    Carrots, sliced, parboiled, and marinated
    Cauliflower buds, marinated
    Beans, red, white, yellow, or green
—In French Dressing*:
    Sliced cooked potatoes with minced scallions
    Cucumbers with dill

Seviche

1 pound fish fillets cut in
    ½-inch cubes or strips
    (whitefish, red snapper,
    haddock, sole, bay scal-
    lops)
1 small onion, chopped
1 small green pepper,
    finely chopped
1 large ripe tomato,
    peeled, seeded, and
    chopped
1 teaspoon salt
⅛ teaspoon freshly
    ground black pepper
½ cup fresh lime juice
    or ⅔ cup fresh lemon
    juice
¼ cup olive oil
⅓ cup tomato juice
½ teaspoon thyme
⅛ teaspoon Tabasco (2 or
    3 dashes)
1 garlic clove, minced
2 tablespoons finely
    chopped parsley

This tangy first course is a kind of pickled fish, the method of marinating in lime or lemon juice having been brought back to Europe from the Orient by Portuguese navigators. The raw pickled fish is surprisingly tender and delicate, but fresh fish must be used to make the dish.

Mix everything together in a glass or porcelain bowl and allow to stand for 4 hours in the refrigerator, or overnight.

Optional garnishes: Thinly sliced Bermuda onion rings, crisped by standing in ice water for an hour; slices of avocado that have been sprinkled with lime or lemon juice to prevent discoloration; chopped pimiento.

Note: Italian parsley, which has more flavor, is better than the curly kind for this dish.

Serves 4–6.

Jambon Persillé (Jellied Ham with Parsley)

3 cups cooked ham in ¼-inch dice
2 envelopes unflavored gelatin
3 cups canned chicken broth, fat removed from top
2 teaspoons tarragon vinegar
1 cup dry white wine
12 whole peppercorns
4 shallots, peeled and chopped
¼ teaspoon thyme
1 small bay leaf
3 parsley sprigs
1 celery stalk with leaves
½ teaspoon dried tarragon
½ cup finely chopped fresh parsley

This is a first course that contrasts well with bland or light stews, particularly those of chicken or veal.

Put the diced ham in a 1½-quart glass bowl in which it can be served, or a 1½-quart mold out of which it can be turned.

Moisten the gelatin with ½ cup broth and the tarragon vinegar. Put remaining broth and the wine in a saucepan with everything else but the chopped parsley. Simmer for 30 minutes. Strain through a moistened and wrung-out kitchen towel and pour onto the moistened gelatin. Stir until gelatin is completely dissolved.

Pour enough of this mixture over the ham to half cover it. Chill the rest until it is firm enough to hold the chopped parsley in suspension, but is still pourable. Stir in the parsley and pour over the ham. Chill until set, at least 2 hours. Serve from the bowl, or unmold by standing the bowl in warm water for a few moments, running a knife around the edge, and turning out on a platter. Serves 6–8.

Crabmeat in Aspic

ASPIC
4 cups canned chicken broth, fat removed from the top
2 envelopes unflavored gelatin
½ cup dry Vermouth
10 whole peppercorns

Moisten the gelatin with ½ cup chicken broth. Put the rest of the broth (3½ cups) in a saucepan with all the other ingredients for the aspic. Bring to a simmer; simmer 30 minutes. Using a moistened and wrung-out kitchen towel strain into the moistened gelatin. Stir until gelatin is dissolved. Taste and add salt if needed; some chicken broths are saltier than others.

Pour about ¼ inch of aspic into each of 6 custard cups. Allow to set. You can hurry it a bit by setting the cups in a pan of ice water.

¼ teaspoon salt
½ teaspoon thyme
½ teaspoon tarragon
1 small bay leaf
1 celery stalk with leaves
4 shallots, peeled and
    chopped
3 parsley sprigs

CRABMEAT MIXTURE
2 cups cooked crabmeat,
    fresh or canned (two
    6½-ounce cans)
¼ cup finely chopped fresh
    parsley
Juice of 1 lemon
¼ teaspoon salt
¼ teaspoon freshly
    ground pepper
Parsley sprigs
2 hard-boiled eggs

Pick over the crabmeat, removing any shell or fibers. Break up any large pieces but do not have it all in very small pieces. Stir in the chopped parsley, lemon juice, salt, and pepper. Break up the parsley sprigs into tiny pieces, moisten with aspic, and lay one in each cup of set aspic. Lay a ¼-inch slice of hard-boiled egg on top of each parsley sprig. Loosely pack the crabmeat mixture into the cups. Pour the rest of the aspic, which should be cool but still pourable, into the cups, making sure it penetrates the crabmeat. Chill for at least 2 hours, until set.

To unmold, set the molds briefly in a pan of warm water; run a knife around the edges; turn each onto a lettuce leaf. Serve with a lemon wedge; garnish with parsley or watercress. Serves 6, or 4 in larger cups.

Cold Shrimp

2 quarts water
2 tablespoons cider
    vinegar
2 teaspoons salt
¼ teaspoon black pepper,
    freshly ground
1 celery stalk with top
4 parsley sprigs
1 teaspoon thyme
1 bay leaf

Shrimp are particularly good before light stews or those served with rice. In a saucepan, place the water and all the other ingredients, except the shrimp. (Tails can be left on the shrimp; they look attractive and make a handle for eating with the fingers.) Bring the water to a simmer, and simmer for 20–30 minutes. Bring to a rapid boil; add the shrimp. When the water comes back to a boil, reduce heat, and allow the shrimp to cook just until they are pink, 3–5 minutes. Do not overcook, or the shrimp will be tough. When they are done, drain them in a colander, pick out and discard the parsley, bay leaf and celery. Spread shrimp out quickly on a paper towel to cool. (They can be rinsed under cold water, but some of the flavor is lost. The bits of

1 pound small shrimp, shelled and deveined (tails may be left on if desired)

seasoning stuck to the shrimp are not unattractive.) Refrigerate when cool. Frozen shelled and deveined shrimp can be done the same way, but they are practically done when the water comes back to a boil. Shrimp separately frozen are better than those frozen in a block. If the latter have to be used, separate them with a fork as they cook. One pound of small shrimp will make a first course for 4. If the shrimp are large, buy 4 or 5 per person, depending on size. Shrimp can be served plain, in a bowl with ice cubes, lemon wedges, and a garnish of parsley sprigs or watercress, or with one of the following sauces:

MAYONNAISE SAUCE

Those who find making mayonnaise a chore may find satisfactory a perked-up unsweetened commercial mayonnaise, thinned with olive oil and sharpened with lemon juice and black pepper. Beat in the oil by drops until the desired texture is reached, add lemon juice ½ teaspoon at a time to gain the desired piquancy, stir in freshly ground black or cayenne pepper, and add a pinch of salt, if necessary.

Mayonnaise, doctored or as it comes, can be pleasantly flavored with Sherry, Port, or Cognac, 1 teaspoon of any of these for each cup of mayonnaise; some people like to add Vermouth. Various herbed mayonnaises offer subtle variations, especially when the herbs are fresh. To each cup of thinned mayonnaise add ½ cup finely chopped parsley or watercress, or ¼ cup each finely chopped parsley and scallions. Using a blender produces a smoother sauce.

GREEN SAUCE
6 tablespoons salad oil
2 tablespoons wine vinegar
½ teaspoon salt
2 teaspoons Dijon mus-

Put all ingredients into a blender and blend until smooth and bright green. This sauce is even more attractive when made by hand, if the herbs and onions are very finely minced; it will look like a beautiful swamp. If fresh basil isn't at hand, use 2 teaspoons dried basil and ¾ cup coarsely chopped watercress, or increase parsley to 1 cup.

tard, or ½ teaspoon dry
mustard
¾ cup coarsely chopped
parsley
¾ cup coarsely chopped
onion
¾ cup coarsely chopped
fresh basil

This makes about 1 cup dressing, enough for as much as 3 pounds shrimp. For 4 people, 1 pound small shrimp is enough as a first course before a stew. If larger shrimp must be used, buy them as you would for a shrimp cocktail, allowing 4–6 per person.

SOUR CREAM AND DILL SAUCE
1 cup sour cream
3 teaspoons chopped
fresh dill, or 1 teaspoon
dried
¼ teaspoon salt
¼ teaspoon white pepper
1 teaspoon lemon juice

Mix all ingredients together. This sauce is also delicious with smoked salmon or crisp vegetables. It can also be made with chives, instead of dill.

Flaming Shrimp

4 tablespoons butter
1 pound small raw
shrimp, shelled and de-
veined
¼ teaspoon salt
3 or 4 grinds of the
peppermill
¼ cup warmed dry Sherry,
preferably Fino or
Amontillado
¼ cup finely chopped
parsley

Flaming dishes are overdone, but this one is simple and delicious, as well as dramatic. It calls for Sherry, which most people believe can't be flamed; the trick is to warm it first. In an electric skillet, chafing dish or a 12-inch enamel-ware skillet, heat the butter to sizzling and add the raw shrimp. Cook, stirring, on a medium flame, until the shrimp are pink and no longer translucent, about 3–5 minutes. Add salt and pepper as the shrimp begin to turn opaque. Ignite the warmed Sherry and pour over the shrimp, taking care not to get burned in the first wild flare. Shake the pan, stir until the flame begins to flicker, add the parsley, stir to distribute it, and begin serving before the last flame dies.

The simplest way to do the flaming is to have the Sherry in a saucepan on a second burner, turned very low. When you are ready to add the Sherry, turn up the flame and tip the saucepan, so that the high flame ignites the fumes from the Sherry. This makes a nice little flurry of action, and requires turning off the high flame that was under the saucepan of Sherry, just as it flares up in the skillet. The dexterity looks quite professional; actually, there's no hurry, because the Sherry will flame along for the better part of a minute.

Port, Vermouth, or any other fortified wine can be used, as can Cognac or other spirits.

Raw chicken livers, about ¾ pound, cut in half, can be done the same way, as can raw bay scallops or quartered sea scallops. The chicken livers, which should be patted dry with a paper towel before being added to the skillet, take no more time than the shrimp, being done as soon as they lose their dark red color. Scallops should be patted dry, too, and are done when they turn opaque, 2–3 minutes.

This recipe serves 4 as a first course. For more people, do the whole recipe in batches, to avoid overcrowding the pan.

Shrimp Chartreuse

2 tablespoons butter
1 pound small shrimp, cooked
1 tablespoon Chartreuse, green or yellow
¼ cup heavy cream, whipped

In an electric skillet or chafing dish, or on top of the stove, heat the butter to the sizzling point. Stir in the shrimp, turning them and shaking the pan for about one minute, to warm them but not cook them any more. Add the Chartreuse, and, still stirring, add the whipped cream. As soon as all is blended, serve immediately. Serves 4.

Other liqueurs like Strega or Irish Mist, or white alcohols like Kirsch or Mirabelle may be substituted for the Chartreuse, for a different flavor.

Cooked crab or lobster can be used in place of shrimp, as can raw bay scallops or quartered sea scallops. The minute or so in the butter is enough to cook the scallops.

Many of the stews in this book are meals in themselves, and require no accompanying dishes. Other, lighter stews would be enhanced by a green vegetable on the side, or by something to soak up the last of the sauce.

Crisp Garlic Bread

Slice Italian or French bread in ¾-inch slices. Place on a cookie sheet in a preheated 350° over for about 10 minutes, until it is lightly brown. Remove and rub each slice with a garlic clove. Paint the top with olive oil and put back in the oven for 5 minutes. This can be done ahead and the bread warmed up at the time of serving. To reheat, put the bread slices in foil, bring up the sides of the foil, not to seal, just to contain the bread. Warm for 5 minutes.

Noodles

Noodles, wide or narrow or in between, go particularly well with stews that have rich sauces. They can be buttered or not, used as a bed for or around the stew, or served as a side dish. They can be varied easily, by adding a tablespoonful or so of poppy or caraway seeds to each ½ pound noodles, cooked, drained, and buttered. Toasted almond slivers or pine nuts, chopped walnuts, or sautéed green peppers are attractive additions, as are pimientos. Of course there's always parsley.

Saffron Rice

2 tablespoons butter
1 tablespoon oil
2 cups long-grain rice
1 medium onion, chopped
4 cups hot canned chicken
   broth
½–1 teaspoon saffron
   threads

Saffron rice has a rich flavor that goes well with light stews. In a 2- or 2½-quart lidded flameproof casserole or sauce-pan heat the butter and oil. Add the rice and onion and cook slowly until the onion is transparent and the rice opaque and both are golden but not brown. The dish may be done ahead to this point.

Add the broth and the saffron, crumbled between the fingers. Stir just once after adding liquid.

Bring to a boil. Turn heat down, cover tightly, and cook over a low flame for 20–25 minutes, or until liquid is absorbed and rice is tender. Fluff with a fork, lifting and separating the grains. Some salt may be needed if there is not enough in the broth.

The rice can be brought to a boil in a flameproof casserole, then be placed in the oven during the absorption time, while the stew finishes cooking or is being reheated. Serves 6.

Risotto

This is a good companion for some stews, particularly Italian ones. Rice is cooked as for Saffron Rice,* with or without the saffron, with ¼–½ cup grated Parmesan cheese and 2 tablespoons melted butter stirred in when the rice is done. Or the cheese may be served in a side dish, to be sprinkled on each serving.

Kasha (Buckwheat Groats)

Kasha is a nice change from the usual starch, but it is a little strong for a delicate stew. It would go with Beef and Sour Cream, or the Basic Browned Beef Stew, with the potatoes left out.

2 cups whole kasha
2 eggs, lightly beaten
2 teaspoons salt
¼ teaspoon pepper
2 tablespoons butter

Mix the kasha thoroughly with the eggs. In a 2- or 2½-quart lidded flameproof casserole, cook the egg and kasha mixture

4 cups hot water

on a very low flame, stirring almost constantly, for 10–20 minutes, or until the grains are separate and brown. At first it sticks a bit and has to be scraped, but soon the grains separate and have to be stirred less often. The dish can be done ahead to this point.

Add the salt, pepper, butter, and hot water, and bring to a simmer. Cover and cook slowly on top of the stove for 20–30 minutes or until water is absorbed and the kasha fluffy.

If the kasha is cooked in a casserole that can go in the oven, cook in the oven for the last ½ hour of the stew's cooking. Serves 6–8.

White-Bean Casserole

2 cups (1 pound) dried
   white beans (Great
   Northern, navy, baby
   lima)
Water to cover
6 cups water
2 teaspoons salt
¼ teaspoon thyme
1 bay leaf
10 whole peppercorns
3 sprigs parsley
1 celery stalk with leaves,
   cut in half
1 medium onion, stuck
   with 3 cloves
2 tablespoons butter
1 medium onion, chopped
¼ cup stew liquid or ¼ cup
   canned beef broth

Wash and pick over beans. Cover with water, bring to a boil, and boil 2 minutes. Remove from heat, cover, and allow to stand for 1 hour.

Drain beans; place in a saucepan with the 6 cups fresh water and all the other ingredients, except the last three. Bring to a boil, turn down, and simmer 1½–2 hours, until beans are tender but not mushy.

Drain the beans, picking out and discarding parsley, celery, onion, and bay leaf.

In a 2- or 2½-quart lidded flameproof casserole, heat the butter and in it slowly cook the onion, until it is golden but not brown. Add the beans. The dish may be done ahead to this point.

Add liquid from the stew, or beef broth. Cover and cook on a low flame for 30 minutes, or place in the oven for the last ½ hour of the stew's cooking time. Serves 6–8.

Matzoh-Meal Dumplings

2 eggs, separated
3 tablespoons soft butter
½ cup hot water or stock
¾ cup matzoh meal
½ teaspoon salt
⅛ teaspoon white pepper
⅛ teaspoon ground ginger
   (optional)

These dumplings are made seperately from the stew. They can stand in the cooking liquid and be added to the stew at serving time.

Beat egg yolks with butter until thick and well blended. Pour in hot water or stock; beat well. Fold in matzoh meal mixed with the salt, pepper, and ginger, if used.

Beat egg whites until stiff but not dry. Fold into dumpling mixture. Chill for 2 hours or longer, the longer the better; the mixture can be left overnight.

Wet hands with cold water and shape mixture gently into 1–1½-inch balls. Drop gently into 2 quarts boiling salted water (1 teaspoon salt per quart of water) or stock. Cover and cook on low flame for 30 minutes if the dumplings are not to be used immediately, or 40 minutes for immediate serving. Do not lift cover during cooking. For later serving, allow the dumplings to cool uncovered in the liquid. At serving time, heat up in their cooking liquid, and add to the stew. Serves 4–6.

Butter Dumplings

3 tablespoons butter
3 eggs
9 tablespoons flour
¼ teaspoon salt
⅛ teaspoon pepper
3- or 4-quart saucepan of
   salted water (1 tea-
   spoon salt per quart of
   water)

These dumplings can be made ahead and added to the stew at serving time, or warmed up in butter and served separately.

Cream the butter until it is light and soft. Beat in the eggs. Stir in the flour, salt, and pepper. This makes more of a batter than a dough. Bring the water to a simmer and make a trial dumpling; if it does not hold together in the simmering liquid, mix a little more flour—1 to 2 teaspoonfuls —into the batter.

Drop batter by teaspoonfuls into the simmering water. Simmer, covered, for 8 minutes. Remove with a slotted spoon to a warm, buttered baking dish. For immediate serving, dot with butter and sprinkle with pepper, or add to the stew, spooning some of the liquid over them. For later serving, reheat in the baking dish lightly covered with foil for 15–20 minutes, or reheat in the stew. Serves 4–6.

Zesty New Potatoes

12–15 small new potatoes
Water barely to cover
1 teaspoon salt per quart
  of water
Juice of 1 lemon
Grated rind of 1 lemon
2 tablespoons butter
¼ cup finely chopped
  parsley
3 or 4 grinds of the
  peppermill

A refreshing treatment of potatoes, Greek in feeling and good with various stews.

Choose small new potatoes with thin skins that break easily, either red or yellow. Scrub them well, and cut off a strip of peel from around the middle of each. Put the potatoes in a lidded flameproof casserole or sauce pan with salted water barely to cover. Cover pan and cook until tender, 30–40 minutes.

Drain, add the lemon juice, grated lemon rind, and butter. Stir, partially cover, and cook on very low flame for about 5 minutes, just long enough for the potatoes to absorb the lemon flavor. Stir in the parsley and pepper, and serve. Serves 4–6, depending on the size of the potatoes.

Red Cabbage and Apple

1 medium red cabbage
  (about 6 cups),
  shredded
2 tablespoons butter
2 medium onions, chopped
2 tart apples, cored and
  sliced
2 tablespoons brown
  sugar
¼ cup dry red wine
¼ cup water

This is a Flemish treatment of red cabbage to go with Dutch, Belgian, or German stews. It has a sweet and sour taste and is not very good with wine but fine with beer.

Trim outer leaves from the cabbage, quarter, and core it. Cut across in ½–¾-inch slices. Do not worry about exact amounts of cabbage; the liquid and seasonings will do for 6–8 cups.

In a 2½- or 3-quart lidded flameproof casserole, melt the butter. Slowly cook the onions and apples in the butter until the onions are limp and transparent. Add the sugar and continue cooking slowly until apples are soft and glazed, about 5 minutes or less. Add the wine, water, and seasonings, and

½ teaspoon salt
¼ teaspoon black pepper
⅛ teaspoon ground cloves
⅛ teaspoon cayenne
   pepper

the cabbage. Bring to a simmer, cover, and cook on very low flame for 1 hour. The cabbage will be very tender. Serves 4–6.

Red Cabbage

1 medium red cabbage
   (about 6 cups shredded)
½ teaspoon salt
½ cup water
1 tablespoon vinegar
Butter

Trim, quarter, and core the cabbage. Cut across in ¼–½-inch slices. Place in a 2½-quart lidded flameproof casserole with the salt, pepper, water, vinegar. Cover and cook about 5 minutes, until cabbage is just tender but still crisp. Drain, butter, and serve. Serves 4–6.

Jim Lee's Chinese Sweet and Sour Pickles

1 medium head cauli-
   flower
2 medium green peppers
4 carrots
3 bunches red radishes
   (or 1 bunch white
   radishes)
2 hot chili peppers
3 quarts boiling water for
   blanching
2 cups sugar
2 cups white vinegar
1 teaspoon salt
1 cup water

These are the pickles that go into Sweet and Pungent Pork. They can also be used as a side dish with Chinese stews. They will keep in the refrigerator for over a year and can be used after standing for one week.

Wash vegetables, peel carrots and white radishes (if used). Scrape off seeds of green peppers, and discard cauliflower stems. Cut all vegetables into bite sizes. Bring 3 quarts water to a boil. Put in the vegetables; turn off heat at once. Allow to stand 2 minutes. Drain off water and spread out the vegetables in one layer to cool and dry. When vegetables are cool, pack them at random in a glass jar or plastic container.

Put the other ingredients into a saucepan; bring to a boil. Remove from stove to cool. When the liquid is cool, pour over the vegetables. Cap the container and store in the refrigerator. Let stand for at least one week before using.

Green Beans

1 pound string beans,
    whole or in 2-inch pieces
1 cup water
½ teaspoon salt
2 tablespoons butter
Toasted nuts (optional)

Trim ends from beans; leave them whole or cut in 2-inch pieces. Put the water and salt in a lidded 1½- or 2-quart saucepan or casserole. Bring to a boil, and add the beans and butter. Cover and cook 10–12 minutes, until beans are tender but still crisp and bright green. If the beans are cut any smaller than 2 inches, they will take even less time to cook. Toasted nuts, almonds, or pine nuts can be added just before serving if desired. Serves 4.

For cooking a larger quantity of beans, put water in the bottom of the pot to the depth of 1 inch; use salt in the proportion of ½ teaspoon per pound of beans. The 2 tablespoons butter will do for 2–3 pounds beans.

Jim Lee's Chinese Green Beans

Wash and trim beans. Break in half if they are too long. Dry thoroughly.

1 pound string beans
1 teaspoon sugar
1 tablespoon cornstarch
2 tablespoons soy sauce
½ cup water or chicken
    stock
¼ cup vegetable oil
⅛ teaspoon salt
2 slices fresh ginger, or a
    dash of Tabasco, or a
    pinch of freshly ground
    black pepper
1 clove garlic, minced
2 tablespoons Sherry

In a bowl, mix together the sugar, cornstarch, soy sauce, and water or stock. Set aside.

Heat a heavy, lidded skillet; put in the oil and salt.

Turn heat to medium, and put in ginger (if it is used) and the garlic. Fry until they are golden, stirring and turning constantly; this is called stir-frying.

Add the beans; stir-fry until beans change to a deeper green color. Add the Sherry, cover, and cook two minutes.

Remove cover, add mixture set aside in bowl, stir-fry until gravy has thickened. Stir in Tabasco or pepper if ginger has not been used. Serves 4.

Broccoli

1 bunch broccoli (about
  2 pounds)
½ teaspoon salt
4 tablespoons butter
4 tablespoons oil

Cut off one inch from the broccoli stems, remove leaves and peel off the tough outer skin. Break off flowerets; split large ones to make them uniform in size. Wash the flowerets and stems; cut the stems on a slant in ⅛-inch slices.

Heat a large skillet, add salt and oil (if necessary adding enough to cover the bottom of the pan by about ⅛–¼ inch). When the fat is hot, put in the broccoli and stir-fry over a medium flame until the broccoli is bright green, about 5 minutes.

Note: Clarified butter (see p. 235) could be used here because it has a higher burning point, and obviates the need for oil. Use 8 tablespoons clarified butter (or enough to cover the bottom of the pan by ⅛–¼ inch). Serves 4–6.

Jim Lee's Chinese Broccoli

Prepare broccoli as in recipe for broccoli above.

1 bunch broccoli (about
  2 pounds)
1 teaspoon sugar
1 tablespoon cornstarch
2 tablespoons soy sauce
½ cup water or canned
  chicken broth
¼ cup vegetable oil
⅛ teaspoon salt
1 clove garlic, minced
2 tablespoons Sherry

In a large bowl, mix together the sugar, cornstarch, soy sauce, and water or chicken broth. Set aside.

Heat a large, lidded skillet, add the oil and salt. Turn heat to medium; add the garlic. When garlic is golden, add the broccoli. Turn up heat and fry for 2 minutes, stirring and turning the broccoli constantly.

Add the Sherry, cover and cook covered for 2 minutes.

Turn down heat, uncover skillet, and add the mixture in the bowl. Stir and cook until gravy has thickened and broccoli is a bright jade green. Serves 4–6.

Braised Endive

Preheat oven to 325°.

12 endives, trimmed and
    washed
Salted water to cover (1
    teaspoon salt per quart
    of water)
¼ cup butter
Juice of ½ lemon
⅛ teaspoon white pepper
Grating of nutmeg

Parboil endives in boiling salted water for 10 minutes, starting them in a rolling boil, then reducing heat and boiling gently. Carefully remove them from the water. Melt butter in a shallow ovenware casserole or baking dish, add the lemon juice, and arrange endives in a single layer, turning them with tongs so that they are coated with the butter. Sprinkle with pepper and a single grating of nutmeg, and place them uncovered in the oven for about an hour. Turn once. When lightly golden, cover and turn off heat. They will keep warm for half an hour, or can be reheated. Serves 6.

SALADS AND
SALAD DRESSING

For most stews, a simple salad of good greens, with plenty of chopped fresh parsley and French dressing, is all that is called for. However, the following are some suggestions for other salad combinations when something more seems to be required:

Beets and endive: drain a can of julienne beets and marinate them for ½ hour in a few spoonfuls of French Dressing.* Cut the endive across in 1-inch slices. Place the endive in the salad bowl with little mounds of the beets here and there, and sprinkle with parsley. At serving time, add a little more dressing and toss. This is to preserve the lovely red-and-white look as long as possible; once the salad is tossed, the beets color the whole thing.

Sliced oranges, scallions, cucumbers, and lettuce: peel, seed, and slice the oranges in thin rounds. Score the cucumbers with a fork and cut in thin slices crosswise. Chop scallions, green and all. Place in the salad bowl on a bed of tender lettuce, such as Boston or Bibb. Sprinkle with parsley and toss with French Dressing.*

Endive and watercress: trim endive and split lengthwise, separating leaves. Wash watercress, trim stems, break up, but do not chop. Toss with French Dressing.*

Boston lettuce, Feta cheese, and black olives: for a meal that does not have a cheese course. Tear the lettuce, crumble Feta cheese into it, and sprinkle with tiny Greek olives. Sprinkle with parsley and toss with French Dressing.*

Garbanzo beans, kidney beans, green pepper, onion, and lettuce: drain and rinse one can garbanzo beans (chick peas) and one can kidney beans. Marinate in ½–¾ cup Sauce Vinaigrette* for at least one hour (the longer the better), with one green pepper, chopped, and one medium red onion in thin rings or chopped. Serve on a bed of lettuce.

Raw mushrooms and parsley: ¾ pound whole button mushrooms, or larger ones coarsely chopped, ½ cup finely chopped parsley, in French Dressing* made with lemon instead of vinegar.

Cucumbers with Sour Cream Dressing*: Peel and halve cucumbers; remove seeds; cut across in 1-inch pieces. Stir in Sour Cream and Dill Sauce,* 1 cup sauce for 2 medium cucumbers. For extra piquancy, add 1 teaspoon horseradish to each ½ cup sauce.

Tomatoes and fresh basil: When tomatoes are at their best and fresh basil is available, a huge platter of perfect tomato slices sprinkled with chopped fresh basil with no dressing at all makes a cool, fresh partner for a stew. If tomatoes are less than perfect, slice them or cut them into wedges, pour on a little French Dressing* and sprinkle with fresh basil.

Spinach and bacon: 1 pound spinach, washed and picked over, stems removed, dried; 2 slices bacon, cooked until crisp, drained and broken into small pieces. Reserve 2 tablespoons bacon fat. Make ½ cup French Dressing* with only 4 tablespoons oil, rather than 6. Add the bacon chips to the spinach. At serving time, heat the bacon fat, pour over the salad, add the French dressing, toss and serve. For a more wilted salad, heat the French dressing with the bacon fat and pour over the spinach. Serve immediately. Serves 4–6.

French Dressing

⅛ teaspoon salt
¼ teaspoon dry mustard
⅛ teaspoon freshly ground
   black pepper
2 tablespoons wine or
   cider vinegar
6 tablespoons olive oil,
   salad oil, or a combi-
   nation

Mix the seasonings with the vinegar; beat in the oil. For a sharper dressing, add a little more vinegar or lemon juice. Makes about ½ cup dressing.

Sauce Vinaigrette

¼ teaspoon salt
⅛ teaspoon freshly ground
   pepper
⅛ teaspoon dry mustard
   (optional)
3 tablespoons wine, tarragon, or cider vinegar
6 tablespoons olive oil,
   vegetable oil, or a combination
¼ teaspoon dried basil
2 tablespoons finely
   chopped fresh parsley
2 tablespoons finely
   chopped green pepper
2 tablespoons finely
   chopped onion
1 teaspoon capers
   (optional)

Vinaigrette sauce is really French Dressing with more vinegar in proportion to the oil, and added herbs and seasonings.

Mix the salt and pepper (and mustard, if used) with the vinegar, beat in the oil and add the rest of the ingredients. This makes about ½ cup sauce, enough for 2–4 cups vegetables to be marinated, depending on how strongly flavored you want the vegetables and how absorbent they are. The vegetables need to stand in the sauce in the refrigerator for at least 2 hours, and they should be stirred occasionally. Taste before serving; a little more salt and vinegar might be needed.

DESSERTS

A hearty stew, preceded by a light first course and followed by salad and cheese, usually requires only a light dessert. Here are some suggestions for light and simple conclusions to such a meal.

Fresh Fruit

A great bowl of assorted fresh fruit makes a perfect dessert. Served toward the end of the cheeses, it makes a nice transition from one course to another, leading pleasantly to coffee and liqueur.

For a lavish feeling, nothing matches huge bowls of a single fruit, when it is at its best at the height of the season, decorated with flowers or small green leaves. Pleasing combinations are green grapes with red carnations or bunches of purple grapes with a couple of white chrysanthemums stuck in among them. Bing cherries or purple plums are striking with yellow roses; for a wedding or anniversary, strawberries decked with sprigs of baby's breath are enchanting.

Some other suggestions for simple fruit desserts:

Generous wedges of cantaloupe, honeydew, or Spanish melon, with Ruby Port to pour on them.

A platter of melon wedges, including watermelon, on a bed of leaves, with wedges of lemon and lime.

Perfect strawberries in a bowl, with their stems left on, to be dipped in sugar and eaten with the fingers.

Oranges, carefully peeled, the seeds removed, sliced into thin rounds. Sprinkle six sliced oranges with 1–2 tablespoons sugar and 2 tablespoons Kirsch. Chill for an hour. Serves 4.

Pears—peel, core, and cube six, sprinkle with lemon juice. Mix with ½–1 cup sour cream, 1 tablespoon sugar, and 2 tablespoons Triple Sec, sprinkle with grated orange peel or fresh ginger or tiny slivers of candied ginger. Serves 4.

Sliced fresh peaches, with a sauce of frozen raspberries. Partially thaw a package of frozen raspberries, put in the blender for a few seconds, strain, and add 2 teaspoons Kirsch.

Sliced or sectioned oranges, with sliced bananas, sprinkled with sugar and shredded coconut.

Fresh strawberries, halved, or quartered if they are very large, sprinkled with sugar and Triple Sec, Cointreau, or Grand Marnier.

Mixed Fruits

Mixtures of cut-up fresh fruits seem particularly refreshing after a stew, to taste and to look at, and the combinations are infinite.

A little sweetening brings out the taste of fruit and judicious use of liqueurs gives extra depth of flavor. Lemon or lime juice adds a refreshing tartness, and a minuscule dash of salt is recommended, to round everything out.

Six or 8 cups of fruit will serve 4 to 6 people. For this quantity, here are some very general suggestions for additions, subject to adjustment according to the acidity of the fruit and personal taste:

1. ¼ cup sugar
    2 tablespoons liqueur:
        Orange-flavored Triple Sec, Cointreau, or Grand

Marnier
Monastery liqueurs like Chartreuse or Strega
Licorice-tasting spirits like Pec, Pernod, or Ricard
Kirsch, Mirabelle, Framboise
Brandy: Cognac, Armagnac, Calvados
Wines: Port, Madeira, Marsala

2. ½ cup honey
Juice of 1 lime

3. ¼ cup sugar
2 tablespoons lemon juice
½ cup orange juice
¼ cup puréed fresh strawberries

4. 1 package frozen sweetened raspberries or strawberries

A few basic principles for successful mixed-fruit desserts:

Chill for at least ½ hour, but not over 1, stirring occasionally.

Many fruits discolor quickly, once cut, particularly pears, peaches, apples, bananas, and avocados. Sprinkle lemon or lime juice over them as they are prepared, or drop into a bowl of water with lemon juice in it, to prevent discoloration. Frozen fruit, with its added preservatives, performs the same function.

Allow frozen fruit to thaw partially before adding fresh fruit, stirring to allow the frozen fruit juice to coat the fruit being added.

Grapefruit should be free from membranes. The easiest way to prepare this is to halve the grapefruit and run a curved, serrated knife around each section, between the membranes.

To prepare whole sections of oranges for compotes, peel the orange with a sharp knife, being sure to remove all the white inner rind, then carefully remove the sections from between the membranes separating them. Grapefruit can be done the same way, for longer pieces than if done the preceding way.

Fruit Compote

FRUIT
2 large pears (2 cups)
2 large apples (2 cups)
Juice of 1 lemon
1 pint strawberries (2
  cups)

This is a fresh-fruit compote with a sauce. Peaches, apricots, plums, seedless grapes, bananas, blueberries, raspberries, melon, and citrus fruits can be substituted for any or part of the suggested fruits. The syrup is enough for 2 more cups of fruit. Keep excess refrigerated in a jar for another time.

SAUCE
1 cup sugar
1½ cups water
⅛ teaspoon salt
¼ teaspoon anise seeds, or
4 cloves, or 2-inch stick
  of cinnamon
Grated rind of 1 lemon

Peel, core, and slice or dice the pears and apples. Drop them into the lemon juice mixed with water to cover, to prevent discoloration. Wash and hull the berries. Drain the pears and apples; mix with the berries.

Put all ingredients into a small saucepan and bring to a boil. Cook for five minutes. Cool, strain over fruit, and chill. Serves 4–6.

Pears in Red Wine

4–6 pears
1 cup sugar
4 whole cloves
2-inch stick of cinnamon
2 cups dry red wine

Choose pears that are firm and not too ripe. Peel them carefully, leaving on stems.

In a lidded flameproof casserole that will nicely hold the pears, put the sugar, spices, and wine. Simmer for five minutes.

Put in the pears, turning to coat with liquid. Bring to a simmer, cover, and place in a 350° oven for 30–40 minutes, depending on size and firmness of the pears. They are done when they are tender but not mushy. Turn them carefully and baste at least twice during the cooking so the pears will be evenly colored.

Cool with the liquid in the smallest bowl that will hold them.

Spoon the liquid over them and turn gently as they cool. When cool, chill for at least an hour. Serve in dessert dishes that will hold some of the liquid. One pear per person.

Stewed Rhubarb and Strawberries

6 stalks rhubarb
¾ cup sugar
1 pint strawberries
Grated orange peel

Wash and trim ends of rhubarb; do not peel unless the skin is very tough. Cut in 1-inch pieces. Place in the top part of a double boiler over boiling water with the sugar. Cover and cook for about 40 minutes, or until rhubarb is tender.

Wash and hull the strawberries; cut in half; add to the rhubarb. Taste for sweetness and add more sugar if needed; cool, and chill. Sprinkle with grated orange peel. Serves 4 by itself, or 6–8 as a sauce for ice cream.

Flaming Fruit

Now that almost every supermarket has its gourmet corner, it's not too difficult to find whole peaches and apricots in fancy jars. Some are brandied; some have ginger added. They make a glamorous quick dessert, when they are drained and flamed.

In an electric frying pan, chafing dish, or large enamelware skillet, melt 2–4 tablespoons butter. Put in the fruit, stir, and turn gently to heat for a minute, but not to cook. Light ¼ cup Cognac, which doesn't need to be warmed but which flames better if it is, and pour over the fruit, guarding against flare by leaning away from the pan. Shake and tip the pan to brandy the fruit thoroughly. Serve while there is still a little flame left. Some of the liquid from the jar can be added, swirled in the hot pan, then poured over. Ice cream can be served with the fruit.

If you flame drained Bing cherries and pour them over scoops of vanilla ice cream, you have Cherries Jubilee. Other liqueurs—Chartreuse, Cointreau, or white alcohols like Kirsch or Mirabelle—can be used, as can Cream Sherry.

Sherbets and Ice Creams

Ice creams and sherbets make fine desserts after a stew. Here are a few suggestions for making them something special.

Toasted shredded coconut makes a delightfully crisp topping for ice cream. For 4, spread out 1 cup of coconut in a 9-by-9-inch cake pan. Place in a 350° oven for 5 minutes or until lightly browned. Some stirring and vigilance are required to make sure the coconut toasts evenly and not too much. It can be toasted ahead, and will stay crisp if it is left spread out and not covered.

About 2 ounces or ¼ cup nuts are enough for a sprinkle on 4 servings. To toast them, spread them in a buttered 9-by-9-inch cake pan and place in a 350° oven for 5 minutes. Stir, and cook 5 minutes more, until the nuts are lightly browned. Crumbs from macaroons or cookies can be quickly made by rolling them out between two sheets of wax paper.

The taste of wines and liqueurs is heightened when poured over ice cream, 1 or 2 teaspoons being a generous amount per serving. Dribble over each portion at the last moment.

Lime or lemon sherbet with cut-up preserved kumquats with a Cream Sherry.
Lime or lemon sherbet with orange liqueur like Triple Sec or Cointreau, with a tiny grating of lemon rind.
Coffee ice cream with a Cream Sherry and toasted coconut.
Coffee ice cream with Ruby Port and walnuts.
Coffee or chocolate ice cream with coffee liqueur like Tia Maria or Kahlúa, and macaroon crumbs.
Vanilla, coffee, or chocolate ice cream with chocolate liqueur like Crème de Cacao, or one with mint flavor as well, like Vandermint.

Vanilla ice cream with Crème de Cassis, or an Amontillado or Cream Sherry, with toasted almonds; or with Strega and pistachio nuts: or with chestnuts in a syrup, preferably the French marrons glacés.

Butter pecan ice cream with honey and Amontillado or Cream Sherry.

Sources for supplies

For Spanish, Mexican, and Latin American specialties, including chorizo, chili powder, Spanish and Hungarian paprika, creamed quince (Dulce de Membrillo), guava paste, dried beans, utensils, etc.
  *Casa Moneo, 210 West 14th St., New York, N.Y. 10011

For Italian foods, cheeses, olives, sausages, pasta, etc.
  *Manganaro Foods Inc., 488 Ninth Ave., New York, N.Y. 10018

For Greek and Middle Eastern specialties.
  Kassos Brothers, 570 Ninth Ave., New York, N.Y.

For Hungarian and some German specialties.
  *Lekvar By The Barrel, 1577 First Ave., New York, N.Y. 10028

For Italian and Near and Middle Eastern foods and spices; ingredients and utensils for food of many nations.
  Trinacria Importing Co., 415 Third Ave., New York, N.Y.

For fresh ginger and Japanese specialties.
  * Katagari & Co., Inc., 224 East 59th St., New York, N.Y. 10022

  Fresh ginger (which is not in the catalogue) is $1.00 per pound, but must be sent the fastest way. Include cost of air mail or special delivery.

For Chinese groceries and utensils.
  Kwong On Lung Co., 686 North Spring St., Los Angeles, California 90012
  Wing Fat Co., 35 Mott Street, New York, N.Y.

For everything in herbs and spices, including fresh ginger, star anise, Five Fragrances Powder, and Hungarian paprika.
  *Aphrodisia, 28 Carmine St., New York, N.Y. 10014
  When ordering fresh ginger, include cost of air mail or special delivery.

* Will fill mail orders; catalogue available.

A Stew Glossary

Butter and Clarified Butter

Many good cooks swear by sweet butter, but if you are used to salted, as is my household, there is no need to switch for the cooking of stews. Butter burns quickly, whether sweet or salt, so if a lot of meat is to be browned, the butter is combined with olive oil or vegetable oil, which has a higher burning point.

Clarified butter does not burn quickly, and makes the addition of oil unnecessary. Once clarified, the butter will keep indefinitely, so it is a good idea to make a fair amount at a time and store it in a jar or crock in the refrigerator.

To clarify a pound of butter, sweet or salt, break it up in a saucepan and heat it very slowly so that it will melt but not brown. When it is all melted and foamy remove it from the heat and place it in the refrigerator. When the butter has hardened, scrape off the foam, lift out the hardened block, and discard the milky sediment in the bottom of the pan. Melt the block again and pour the now-clarified butter into a storage receptacle. The hardened foam can be used with vegetables.

To clarify a little butter when some is needed, melt slightly more butter than is called for. When it is foamy but not brown, skim off the foam and carefully pour off the butter from the milky sediment in the bottom of the pan. Clarified butter is great for sautéing croutons or large quantities of mushrooms, and for anything that calls for cooking in butter alone. The flavor is properly buttery and there is less danger of the off taste of burning.

Casseroles and Baking Dishes

See Author's Note at beginning of book for information on sizes and kinds of casseroles.

To clean the inside of enameled ironware casseroles, which tend to discolor with time and use, fill the casserole with warm water and ½ cup household bleach and allow to stand overnight. A paper towel large enough to hang over the edge and soaked in the liquid will bleach the rim. If the lid is put on top, the soaked paper towel will bleach stain on the edge of the pot lid as well.

Cooling a Stew

A warm stew should never be tightly covered. Not only will it continue to cook, but there is a good chance it will spoil. If a stew is cooked ahead of time, for later reheating, cool it as quickly as possible by leaving it uncovered in a cool place, or by putting a couple of inches of cold water in the sink and standing the stew in it. Cover and refrigerate only when it is cool. If solids stick up out of the stew, spoon some sauce over to keep them from drying out.

Deglazing, or Rinsing the Pan

The method of browning meat and onions in a skillet and then removing them to a casserole used throughout this book eliminates one step beloved by cooks. This is the "Rinsing of the Browning Pan" to incorporate into the stew any goodies at the bottom of the pan.

Rinsing is not mentioned in the recipes because it would need the qualifying phrase "if not too burned." After the grease has been poured off, stuck bits in the skillet, dissolved in a little water or wine, can be an enrichment of a stew. If a lot of meat and onions have been browned in the pan, however, some stuck bits are apt to be burned, and what you add to the stew is a burned taste.

You will have to judge whether to deglaze the skillet or not. Usually, the browning of 2 pounds of meat, plus the onions, will be done quickly enough to avoid burning. Rinsing the pan with ½ cup of the water or wine called for in the recipe will give a nice added flavor and color to the stew.

Degreasing

This is a tiresome but essential step in finishing a stew. The easiest way to do this is to cool the stew, then refrigerate it until the fat hardens, at which point it can be lifted off. This is a good reason for making a stew a day before it is to be served, so you can skip all those "tip pot and skim off fat" directions.

For same-day serving, the liquid fat has to be skimmed off one way or another. Tipping the pot concentrates the fat in a small area. When you have removed all you can with a spoon, the last bits can be blotted up with paper towels. For a stew with a lot of fat, a bulb baster to suck up the fat will be helpful.

Expanding a Recipe

When expanding a recipe, start with the original amount of fat called for, because you will be browning in batches. Add more fat as you go on. For a very large stew, you can brown a batch in the oven (see p. 90) while you are doing another on the top of the stove. Or you can brown the meat in more than one skillet, though using more than two can be hectic. In any case, it is important to keep the pieces well spaced apart in the pan, because if they are crowded together they will steam rather than brown.

The liquid must still "barely cover," if that is what is called for. Quantity may not increase in the same proportion as the meat. Seasonings should be doubled cautiously, and you should taste as you go. A single bay leaf may prove enough for a doubled recipe, and salt might be increased by half as much again to start with, more being added later.

To reduce a recipe, follow the same procedures. But it is usually easier to make the recipe in its original quantity and store what is left over for another day. Or ask another guest.

Fixing Up a Stew

For even the best of cooks, a stew will occasionally turn out to be something less than the delectable dish it should be. First give it a gentle stir, and then decide what it needs.

Color

If the problem is color, it is easily solved. An unbrowned stew with eggs and cream in it should be light and creamy in color; if it is not, more cream might be enough to fix it. Judicious use of vegetable food coloring is possible too. Yellow liquid coloring, the kind that comes in little bottles for coloring Easter eggs, can be added, a drop at a time, until the right color is arrived at.

An unbrowned stew that does not have cream or cream and egg in it may be a rather drab color, neither creamy nor brown. In this case a little brown coloring helps. Commercial coloring agents that are advertised as gravy makers have too much flavor and will change the taste of the stew. Use one that is as unflavored as possible. To be sure of not imparting any unwanted flavor, make your own coloring with liquid food coloring. To make enough brown coloring for 2 cups of stew liquid, mix together in a tablespoon: ¼ teaspoon red, ¼ teaspoon yellow, ⅛ teaspoon green, that is: 1 part red, 1 part yellow, ½ part green.

For stews with meat that is browned first but that are not as brown as you would like them to be, use the same formula. Browned stews that have cream or sour cream added to them should be a lovely golden beige. If they are not, brown coloring is called for. Stews with tomatoes in any form, especially if they also include paprika, will usually be an attractive reddish brown, but a little brown coloring, with an extra drop of red and a drop of yellow, can be used in them to accent the color. A traditional method for coloring browned stews is to add sugar (1 tablespoon for 3 pounds meat, a little less for 2 pounds) after the browning, before the flouring, tossing until the sugar is caramelized.

Too thick

Add hot water, ½ cup at a time, for a stew that has cooked down too much, or if you just want more gravy. Water is added because it is water that has cooked away; adding stock will make the stew too salty; adding wine will make it taste too winy. Always taste after adding water, and add salt and pepper if needed.

Too thin

First remove the solids for easier coping, and to avoid over-cooking the meat and vegetables. The sauce can be strained at this point for a more elegant appearance. Then taste the sauce. If it is not quite salty enough, or otherwise not strong enough in flavor, it can be reduced and concentrated by boiling briskly for a few minutes. If the flavor is just right, only thickening is called for. To thicken, mix until smooth 2 tablespoons flour with 4 tablespoons water; slowly stir into the simmering liquid, a little at a time. Cook 2–3 minutes after each addition until the stew is the desired consistency. If more flour is needed, add more but always mixed with water. Cornstarch makes a more transparent thickening; it is twice as strong as flour—1 tablespoon cornstarch mixed with 2 tablespoons water will thicken as much as 2 tablespoons flour. Another way of thickening is to mix equal amounts of flour and butter with fingers or a fork. Start with 2 tablespoons flour and 2 tablespoons butter, adding a little at a time to the simmering liquid until the stew is the desired consistency.

Too much liquid

A stew looks most appetizing when the meat shows above the sauce. Occasionally, in the mysterious way of stews, the liquid increases in the cooking rather than reducing and a stew that has had liquid to "barely cover" ends up with even more liquid and looks drowned. Sometimes this is to be expected, as in the case of stews with large quantities of onions, which produce liquid as they cook, or when there are fresh tomatoes, which do the same. If you end up with too much sauce that is otherwise right in taste and consistency, simply remove enough so that the stew has the proper amount. Serve it in a bowl for those who want more gravy. If it is too thick or too thin, follow the procedures above.

Freezing Stew

To freeze a stew, first cool it quickly and thoroughly. The quickest way is to run a couple of inches of cold water into the sink, put in a tray of ice cubes, and set in the uncovered casserole. Once cooled, the stew can be stored in plastic containers, but leave at least ½ inch space above the stew to allow for expansion. Spoon sauce over any bits that protrude.

If a stew contains the following ingredients they are better cooked and added to the stew when it is being reheated:

potatoes	lima beans	spinach
rice	green peppers	peas
noodles	cabbage	corn
dumplings		

White stews should have their finish of cream and eggs added after reheating, not before being frozen.

Fish stews are better when the sauce is frozen alone, the fresh fish being added for the short time of cooking after the sauce has been reheated.

Stews with beans can be frozen.

Stews with a lot of liquid, to which vegetables are added for the last half hour or so of cooking, are better when frozen without the vegetables. The vegetables can be added when the stew comes to a simmer, during the reheating.

Frozen stews without a lot of liquid can be reheated in the oven. Place the stew in a partially covered casserole in a 325° oven for about 1 hour. After 20–30 minutes the frozen block can be broken and spread. The lid should not be put on tightly because the condensation of water under the lid can dilute and spoil the stew, but without a lid at all the top of the stew would dry out.

Top-of-the-stove stews and soup-stews can be thawed and reheated in about 45 minutes over a low flame, in a partially covered casserole or saucepan. At the beginning check often to be sure the bottom of the frozen block is not sticking and burning.

Frozen stews should be used within four weeks.

Garlic

In this book's recipes, garlic is often mashed with salt and added with the other seasonings. Sometimes the directions call for mincing or chopping the garlic and adding it with the onions, to be cooked until golden but not brown. In other cases, it is cooked briefly in oil and then removed, merely flavoring the fat. There are reasons for these apparent inconsistencies.

Garlic browns quickly, imparting a strong taste when it does, and the taste of browned garlic is not desirable. When garlic is cooked briefly in fat, it is usually either whole or smashed, depending on how much garlic taste is wanted: either way it is removed. When garlic is minced and cooked with onion in the fat, it adds flavor without browning, and can be left in with the onions. Mashed with salt, the garlic, though strong, is in very small particles and becomes part of the general seasoning. In some cases, when the sauce is to be strained, the garlic is used unpeeled, or smashed slightly to release more flavor. Garlic can be a strong flavor, or a subtle one, and these various ways of using it give the cook the needed control.

Herbs

Use fresh herbs in place of dried ones whenever you can, 1 tablespoon fresh herbs equaling ½ teaspoon dried. Many herbs and spices keep their flavor better if they are kept in the refrigerator, particularly curry powder, fresh bulk Hungarian paprika, fresh chili powder, and cayenne pepper.

Leftovers

Leftover stew, arranged in a casserole or baking dish, along with the leftover starch (rice, potatoes, noodles) and accompanying vegetables, and refrigerated, makes a complete meal for another time, requiring only a fresh garnish.

Leftover anchovies and pimientos should be removed from their cans before storage. They can be refrigerated for about a week, and will keep better if covered with a film of oil. They may also be wrapped in foil or plastic and frozen, but will lose some of their texture.

Tomato paste should also be transferred from its can to a nonmetallic container and filmed with oil before storage.

Egg whites, left over when stews are thickened with yolks, can be frozen and kept almost indefinitely. They can be frozen in small plastic bags, 2 in a bag, for use in a soufflé. If you freeze several together and forget how many there are, 1½ tablespoons equals 1 egg white.

Fresh ginger will keep for a few days in the refrigerator wrapped in foil or plastic. For longer storage, keep it in a jar of Sherry.

Meat, Cuts for Stew

BEEF Cuts of beef for stewing can be confusing because they vary in appearance and name, not only from one part of the country to another, but even from store to store. New names are constantly being invented for cuts of meat, particularly beef. It can help if you know a little about the animal and what to ask for, no matter what the regional, fashionable, or just plain gimmicky local name is. Don't let the butcher talk you out of a cheaper cut if that is what you want; the cheaper cut will probably be a better one for stew.

Except for rump and round, which will be dealt with later, stewing beef comes mostly from the forequarter. The most familiar and most universal cut for stew is *chuck*. But there are chuck roasts, chuck steaks, chuck fillet steaks, and packaged stewing meat labeled simply ''Stewing Beef, Chuck.'' If you buy chuck fillet steaks thick enough and cut them up yourself, you will have good stewing meat, although there is some waste unless you use the bones for stock. Regular chuck steaks or chuck roasts will be apt to have some less tender parts, as will the so-called stewing chuck. The best and cheapest in the end is boneless *middle chuck,* which is merchandised as ''Chuck Fillet.'' But to get this, without some bits of neck or blade, which can be stringy, you have to have a good butcher you can trust. It helps to know that what you want is the real middle chuck, and to ask for it with authority. Even good supermarket butchers will give you what you want, but you may have to order it ahead.

The end pieces from sirloin and porterhouse steaks are marvelous for stew. Instead of having them ground, freeze them and save them for stew.

Boned shoulder, often called *cross ribs,* is another good cut for stew. *Shank* and *shin* are inexpensive cuts which can be bought boned or unboned. There is a variety of textures in the pieces and they require long slow cooking in plenty of liquid.

Slabs of meat from over the ribs, the thin strips from the ends of the ribs of a rib roast, are excellent for stewing, and are called *top rib,* or *top of rib.* Also good are strips from the breast. Going toward the back of the animal from the shank, and getting progressively fatter, there is *brisket,* followed by *short plate.* The first cuts of brisket nearest the shank are excellent, but again, you need a good butcher to be sure you are getting what you ask for.

Flanken is a favorite stewing cut for many European cooks when it is well marbled with fat, and grainy; it comes from the first cuts under the shoulder and on the first ribs. Second cuts are called *short ribs*—good too, but bonier.

Two cuts very good for stew, but not ordinarily sold as such in regular butcher ships or supermarkets, are *corner pieces* and *deckle.* They are "restaurant cuts," usually sold only wholesale. Corner pieces, often used for restaurant browned stews, are the first cuts from the short plate, nearest the brisket. *Deckle* is an overall term for the thin strips of meat over the ribs and the thinner ones from under the ribs, very good for boiled beef, if you can get it.

Rump and *round,* from the hindquarter, are sometimes used for stew, but they lack the marbling of fat, and tend to be dry. However, in slices or in small cubes, and cooked in plenty of liquid, they have a firm texture that many people enjoy.

LAMB *Boned shoulder* is the best cut for lamb stew. Neck is marvelous for taste and texture, but unless you remove the many little bones before serving, a messy job, it does not make as attractive a stew as does the boneless shoulder.

VEAL *Boned shoulder* is best for veal stew, too, except when slices from the leg are called for.

PORK For pork stews, again it is *boned shoulder,* although other cuts are equally good. *Boned loin* is more expensive, but if you have the bones cut up and use them too, you will not feel so extravagant. The ribs can also be frozen, and roasted for a tasty appetizer some other time. *Fresh ham* can also be used, but it usually comes in a large piece, and you might have to freeze some for later use.

The cuts suggested with the recipes in this book are based on our preferences, and ease of availability. But tastes differ and you may want to experiment with other cuts than those given. The timing will differ with different cuts, but once you know that a stew is done when it is tender, *however long or short the time,* you can feel free to use any cut you wish.

Onions

To peel all those little white onions called for in so many recipes, cut off tops and bottoms, pour boiling water over them, allow to stand for 2–3 minutes, drain, and rinse with cold water. Skins will slip off easily. Make a small cross cut in the root end for more even cooking and less separation.

Slice or chop onions with a stainless-steel knife; nonstainless knives discolor onions.

Onion odor can be removed from hands by rinsing in cold, not hot, water, and rubbing with salt.

Reheating the Stew

The reason for bringing the stew to room temperature before reheating is not only to avoid cracking the enamel on the casserole, if the stew has been frozen, but also to avoid the formation of steam under the lid or foil, which is not good for the stew. In fact, the stew should not be too tightly covered while it is coming to room temperature, and the lid or covering should be checked before the casserole is placed in the oven, to make sure there are no drops of water on it. There is a good argument for doing the entire reheating with the vessel only loosely covered, as for a frozen stew. Two of the recipes in the book specifically call for partial covering during reheating: Arni Prassa* and Mediterranean Chicken.*

Seasoning

Phrases like "correct seasoning" or "check seasoning" mostly mean adding salt and pepper. The amounts called for in the recipes are usually minimum, because it is easier to add more than remove an excess. In the case of stews containing hot seasonings like cayenne, crushed red peppers, or Tabasco, the phrase means adding as much more hotness as you can stand.

When a stew contains orégano or chili powder, or something like anise or fennel seeds, you might like to increase them for more of that particular taste. Also, if herbs and spices are stale, the amount specified may be too little. When correcting seasoning to taste, add small amounts at a time, stir, and cook a moment or two before tasting again. Repeat the process until the taste seems right to you.

If a stew tastes too salty, it could be that it has cooked down too much. First try adding hot water in ½-cup amounts to bring the liquid back to its original level. If there is too much salt in the stew through a mistake in measuring, decide to have potatoes as accompaniment and cook them in the stew. Cut the potatoes in large or small pieces depending on the time needed; they should be done when the stew is. Another method of decreasing saltiness is to remove the solids and grate a potato into the sauce, simmer for about 8 minutes, and then strain out the potato; it will have absorbed some of the salt.

Simmering

"To keep in a heated condition just below boiling-point," is the way the Oxford Dictionary defines simmering. This is not as helpful as the definition related to "feelings, tendencies, etc.": "To be in a state of gentle activity; to be on the verge of becoming active or breaking out." The definition related to "persons, etc." has a clue: "To be in a state of suppressed excitement or agitation." Larousse defines simmering as "the slight quivering of a liquid just before it comes to the boil." Rhapsodic chefs have described a simmering liquid as "smiling."

In stew cookery, the liquid is usually brought to a boil and then turned down to a simmer. There is no trouble recognizing a boil, even a gentle boil. The simmer is below the gentle boil and above the point where nothing is happening at all. There should be movement, but no violent activity on the surface, nothing more than an occasional gentle plop or the sighing break of a bubble.

The problem is to maintain the simmer, and it is almost impossible on top of the stove. First, the liquid goes from simmering to not doing anything. Then, when the flame is turned up a hair, it goes into a gentle boil. Since slow, even cooking is required, oven cooking is suggested in this book.

Temperatures vary from oven to oven, so you will have to experiment with your oven to find the right temperature.

We suggest 325° as a starting point and then adjustment down from there, to the point where there is agitation but not bubbling when the lid of the pot is removed.

If you must use the top of the stove, turn down the heat as low as possible and raise the pot slightly, so that it does not come too close to the flame. Asbestos pads are useless. There is a gadget resembling a covered, upside-down pie plate with holes around the edge, which works fairly well, but still the pot needs constant checking. A rack can be used, in the same way, but is equally unsatisfactory.

Electric frying pans and cooking pots are fine for chicken or fish stews, which are quickly done, but for long-cooking stews they do not maintain the heat steadily enough. The heating element goes on when the stew gets too cool and goes off when it gets too hot, and there is too much starting and stopping.

Stock

For some of the stews in this book, recipes are given for homemade stocks, but many cooks are satisfied with canned beef or chicken broth. Consommé is not recommended because it is too sweet, while all the powdered stocks have a taste that can get to be too familiar because of their dominant flavor, and therefore can taste unpleasant. Also, the salt content in powdered stocks is a factor to beware of; chances are it will make the stew too salty, if other salt is called for. Canned broths are salted, too, and if you choose to use them in place of water, check the taste before adding salt.

Beef- and chicken-broth cans are irritatingly unstandardized, coming in crazy sizes—10½ ounces, 13 ounces, 13¾ ounces—all less than 2 cups, the 16 ounces many recipes call for. It is practical to have several cans of both chicken and beef broth on hand, in case you plan to cook a stew. Leftover broth will keep in the refrigerator for three or four days, and it can be frozen in plastic containers. Take care to measure before freezing, and mark the container; it is a good idea to freeze in 1- and 2-cup lots.

Timing

It is difficult to predict the length of time a stew will take to cook. The quality, and cut of meat and the size of pieces, as well as the idiosyncrasies of stoves, all make differences in cooking times. No matter what the predicted cooking time, the stew is done when it is fork tender, and further cooking will not improve it.

In general, beef takes the longest time to stew, veal the next-longest, and lamb the least. There is no getting around it, some vigilance is necessary to produce a good stew, not only to make sure it is not overdone, but to check the cooking liquid, which will sometimes need augmenting.

Pronunciation Guide

Abbacchio alla Ciociara   ah-*bahk*-kyo ahla choh-*chah*-rah
Abbacchio alla Romana   ah-*bahk*-kyo ahla ro-*mah*-na
Äigo Sau   *eye*-go *sah*-oo
Arni Prassa   *ar*-nee *prah*-sa
Beef Stroganoff   beef-*strow*-gan-off
Blanquette d'Agneau à l'Ancienne   blah[n]-ket danyoh ah lo[n]-see-yen
Blanquette de Veau   blah[n]-ket duh vo
Boeuf à la Hongroise   buhff a lah awng grwahz
Boeuf Bourguignon   buhff boor-geen-yaw[n]
Bouillabaisse   bwee-yah-bess
Carbonada Criolla   car-bo-*nah*-dah cree-*oh*-yah
Carbonnades Flamandes   car-boh-nahd flah-mahnd
Carne all' Ungherese   *car*-neh al uhng-geh-*reh*-seh
Chicken Cacciatore   chicken cah-cha-*tow*-reh
Chicken Paprikash   chicken *pap*-ree-kahsh
Chili con Carne   *chee*-lee con *car*-neh
Coq au Vin Rouge   coke koh va[n] rouge
Creole Jambalaya   cray-ole zjam-bah-*lie*-ah
Daube de Boeuf à la Provençale   dobe duh buhff a lah pro-vo[n]-sahl
Etuvée de Veau au Vin Blanc   ay-tew-vay duh vo oh va[n] blah[n]
Fricassee of Chicken   frih-cah-say of chicken
Hâché   ahsh-ay
Lamb and Bean Khoreshe   lamb and bean ko-*resh*
Lamb Pilaf   lamb *pea*-laff
Lapin aux Prunes   lah-pa[n] oh prewn
Maiale Affogato   my-*ahl*-eh ahf-oh-*gah*-toe
Manzo Garofanato   *mahnt*-zo gah-roh-fah-*nah*-toe
Navarin Printanier   nav-ah-ra[n] pra[n]-tah-nyay
Ökörfarok Ragú   *oke*-ore-fah-rawk rah-*goo*
Plain Old Chicken and Dumplings   plane ohl chickun un *dump*-lins
Pot-au-Feu   poe toe fuh
Puchero Criolla   poo-*cheh*-ro cree-*oh*-yah
Ragoût de Boeuf Bordelais   rah-goo duh buhff bor-duh-lay
Ratatouille   rah-tah-too-ee
Solianka   sol-*yahn*-kah
Soupe au Pistou   soup oh pea-stoo
Stifado   stee-*fah*-doe
Stufatino   stoo-fah-*tee*-no
Szekely Gulyàs   *zeh*-keh-lee *gool*-yahsh
Ternera al Jerez   tare-*neh*-rah al heh-*reth*
Veal Paprikash   veal *pap*-ree-kahsh
Wienersaft Gulyàs   *veen*-er-saft *gool*-yahsh
Yoghurt Khoreshe   *yo*-gurt ko-*resh*

Bracketed [n] is only half-pronounced.

Index

Abbacchio alla Ciociara, 81
Abbacchio alla Romano, 83
Anchovies, leftover, 242
Antipasto, 205
Appetizers
  Antipasto, 205
  bread sticks with prosciutto, 203
  Chicken Consommé
    Hot, 204
    Jellied, 204
  Chicken livers, flaming, 212
  Crabmeat in Aspic, 208
  dried beef as, 203
  Hors d'Oeuvre Varié, 206
  Hummus, 202
  Jambon Persillé, 208
  Mock Soufflé on Toast, 202
  Nuts, 203
  Oeufs Durs Mayonnaise, 205
  Salmon, smoked, 205
  Seviche, 207
  Shrimp
    Chartreuse, 212
    Cold, 209
    Flaming, 211
  Vegetable combinations, raw, 201
Apple, Red Cabbage and, 217
"Armenian" stew
  Sweet and Sour Meatball Stew, 148
Argentinian
  Carbonada Criolla, 59
  Puchero Criolla, 145
Arni Prassa, 90
Aspic, Crabmeat in, 208

Basic
  Browned Beef Stew, 31
  Unbrowned Beef Stew, 131

Bean(s)
  dried, 90
  Green, 219
    Jim Lee's Chinese, 219
  kidney, 62, 222
  White
    Casserole, 215
    Khoreshe, Lamb and, 88
Beard, James, 79
Beef
  Boeuf à la Hongroise, 49
  Beouf Bourguignon, 46
  Borscht, Russian, 141
  Carbonada Criolla, 59
  Carbonnades Flamandes, 37
  Carne all'Ungherese, 51
  Chili con Carne, 62
  Collops, 133
  cuts for stew, 243–44
  Daube de Boeuf à la Provençale,
    138
  dried, as appetizer, 203
  Five Fragrances, 149
  Hâché, 35
  Manzo Garofonato, 53
  Meatball Stew, Sweet and Sour, 148
  Peking Style, Stewed Shin, 64
  Pot-au-Feu, 135
  Puchero Criolla, 145
  Ragoût de Boeuf Bordelais, 44
  Short-Rib Stew, 33
  with Sour Cream, 39
  Stew
    Basic Browned, 31
    Basic Unbrowned, 131
  Stifado, 55
  Stroganoff, 41
  Wienersaft Gulyàs, 143
  see also Oxtails

Beer
  Brussels Pork Stew, 93
  Carbonnades Flamandes, 37
Beets
  and endive salad, 222
  see also Russian Beef Borscht
Belgian
  Brussels Pork Stew, 93
  Carbonnades Flamandes, 37
Blanquette d'Agneau à l'Ancienne, 79
Blanquette de Veau, 154
Boeuf
  à la Hongroise, 49
  à la Provençale, Daube de, 138
  Bourguignon, 46
Borscht, Russian Beef, 141
Bouillabaisse, 176
Braised Endive, 221
Bread
  Crisp Garlic, 213
  sticks with prosciutto, 202
Broccoli, 220
  Jim Lee's Chinese, 220
Browned Beef Stew, Basic, 31
Brunswick Stew, 171
Brussels Pork Stew, 93
Brussel sprouts, see Brussels Pork
  Stew
Buckwheat Groats, 214
Butter
  to clarify, 80, 235
  Dumplings, 216

Cabbage, Red, 218
  and Apple, 217
Canadian
  Oxtail Ragoût, 193
Cantaloupe, 225

Carbonada Criolla, 59
Carbonnades Flamandes, 37
Carne all'Ungherese, 51
Casseroles
 how to clean, 236
 selecting, 18–19
Central European
 Oxtail Ragoût, 193
Cherries Jubilee, 229
Chick-pea spread, 202
 see also Garbanzo beans
Chicken
 Brunswick Stew, 171
 Cacciatore, 111
 Consommé
  Hot, 204
  Jellied, 204
 Coq au Vin Rouge, 103
 and Dumplings, Plain Old, 166
 Fricassee of, 169
 Mediterranean, 108
 Paprikash, 112
 Tarragon, 106
Chicken livers, flaming, 212
Chili con Carne, 62
Chinese
 Broccoli, Jim Lee's, 220
 Five Fragrances Beef, 149
 Green Beans, Jim Lee's, 219
 Lion's Head, 100
 Stewed Shin Beef, Peking Style, 64
 Sweet and Pungent Pork, 98
 Sweet and Sour Pickles, Jim Lee's,
  218
Clam(s)
 in Bouillabaisse, 176
 Chowder
  Manhattan, 180
  New England, 179
 Seafare Stew, 187
Cocktails, Margarita, 62
Coconut, to toast shredded, 230
Cod
 in Bouillabaisse, 176
 in Sailors' Stew, 118
Cognac, to flame, 48, 229
Collops, 133
Color of stew, to improve, 238–39
Compote, Fruit, 228
Consommé
 Hot Chicken, 204
 Jellied Chicken, 204

Coq au Vin Rouge, 103
Crabmeat
 in Aspic, 208
 see also Shrimp Chartreuse
Creole Jambalaya, 183
Cucumbers
 with Sour Cream and Dill Sauce, 205
 with Sour Cream Dressing, 223
Curry, Lamb, 159

Daube de Boeuf à la Provençale, 138
Deglazing, 236
Degreasing, 237
Desserts
 Fruit
  Compote, 228
  Flaming, 229
  Fresh, 225
  Mixed, 226
  Pears in Red Wine, 228
  Rhubarb and Strawberries,
   Stewed, 229
 Sherbets and Ice Creams, 230
Dips, vegetables with, 201
Dumplings
 Butter, 216
 Matzoh-Meal, 216
 Plain Old Chicken and, 166
Dutch beef stew
 Hâché, 35

Eels
 in Bouillabaisse, 176
 in Sailors' Stew, 118
Eggplant
 Ratatouille I, 124
 Ratatouille II, 126
Eggwhites, leftover, 242
Eggs with mayonnaise, hard-boiled,
 205
Endive, braised, 221
Endive and watercress salad, 222
English beef stew
 Collops, 133
Expanding a recipe, 237

Fat, removing liquid, 237
Fish
 Aïgo-Sau, 174
 Bouillabaisse, 176
 Sailors' Stew, 118
 Seafare Stew, 187

Seviche, 207
 see also Salmon
Five Fragrances Beef, 149
Fixing up a stew, 238–40
Flaming
 Cognac, 48, 229
 Sherry, 211
Flemish beef stew
 Carbonnades Flamandes, 37
Flounder
 in Bouillabaisse, 176
French
 Aïgo-Sau, 174
 Beef Stroganoff, 41
 Blanquette d'Agneau à l'Ancienne,
  79
 Blanquette de Veau, 154
 Boeuf Bourguignon, 46
 Boeuf à la Hongroise, 49
 Chicken Tarragon, 106
 Coq au Vin Rouge, 103
 Daube de Boeuf à la Provençale,
  138
 Dressing, 224
 Etuvée de Veau au Vin Blanc, 67
 Lapin aux Prunes, 115
 Navarin Printanier, 76
 Pot-au-Feu, 135
 Ragoût de Boeuf Bordelais, 44
Fricassee of Chicken, 169
Fruit(s)
 for dessert, fresh, 225
 Flaming, 229
 Mixed, 226

Garbanzo (Bean(s))
 Casserole, 147
 Hummus, 202
 and kidney beans, green pepper,
  onion, and lettuce salad, 223
Garlic, cooking, 241–42
Garlic Bread, Crisp, 213
Ginger, fresh
 Jim Lee's Chinese Green Beans, 219
 Lion's Head, 100
 and Pears, 226
 Stewed Shin Beef, Peking Style, 64
 to store, 242
 Sweet and Pungent Pork, 98
Grapefruit, to prepare, 227
Greek
 Arni Prassa, 90
 Stifado, 55

Green Beans, 219
   Jim Lee's Chinese, 219
Green Sauce, 210

Hâché, 35
Haddock
   in Bouillabaisse, 176
   in Sailors' Stew, 118
Hake
   in Bouillabaisse, 176
Halibut
   in Bouillabaisse, 176
   in Sailors' Stew, 118
Ham
   with Parsley, Jellied, 208
   prosciutto, 202
Herbs, storing, 242
Honeydew melon, 225
Hors d'Oeuvre Varié, 206
Hummus, 202
Hungarian
   Boeuf à la Hongroise, 49
   Carne all 'Ungherese, 51
   Chicken Paprikash, 112
   Ökörfarok Ragú, 121
   Szekely Gulyàs, 95
   Veal Paprikash, 69

Ice Creams, 229–30
Indian
   Lamb Curry, 159
Irish Stew, 157
Ironware casseroles, to clean enameled, 236
Italian
   Abbacchio alla Ciociara, 81
   Abbacchio alla Romano, 83
   Carne all'Ungherese, 51
   Chicken Cacciatore, 111
   Maiale Affogato, 163
   Manzo Garofonato, 53
   Mediterranean Chicken, 108
   Stufatino, 71
Italian pork stew
   Maiale Affogato, 163

Jambon Persillé, 208
Jim Lee's Chinese
   Broccoli, 220
   Green Beans, 219
   Sweet and Sour Pickles, 218
   see also Chinese

Kasha, 214
Kidney beans
   Chili con Carne, 62
   in salad, 223

Lamb
   Abbacchio alla Ciociara, 81
   Abbacchio alla Romano, 83
   Arni Prassa, 90
   and Bean Khoreshe, 88
   Blanquette d'Agneau à l'Ancienne, 79
   Curry, 159
   cuts for stew, 245
   Irish Stew, 157
   Navarin Printanier, 76
   Pilaf, 85
Lapin aux Prunes, 115
Lee, Jim, see Jim Lee's Chinese
Leftovers, 242
Lemon Veal, 152
Lettuce, see Salads
Lianides, Leon, 90, 108
Lion's Head, 100
Liver, see Chicken livers, flaming
Lobster, see Shrimp Chartreuse

Maiale Affogato, 163
Manhattan Clam Chowder, 180
Manzo Garofonato, 53
Margarita cocktails, 62
Matzoh-Meal Dumplings, 216
Mayonnaise Sauce, 210
Meatball Stew, Sweet and Sour, 148
Mediterranean
   Bouillabaisse, 176
   Chicken, 108
   Daube de Boeuf à la Provençale, 138
   Soupe au Pistou, 196
   vegetable stew
      Ratatouille I, 124
      Ratatouille II, 126
Melon for dessert, 225
Mexico
   Chili con Carne, 62
Middle Eastern
   Lamb and Bean Khoreshe, 88
   Lamb Pilaf, 85
   Yoghurt Khoreshe, 57
Mock Soufflé on Toast, 202

Mullet
   in Bouillabaisse, 176
Mushrooms and parsley salad, raw, 223

Navarin Printanier, 76
New England Clam Chowder, 179
Noodles, 213
Nuts
   as appetizer, 203
   to toast, 230

Oeufs Durs Mayonnaise, 205
Ökörfarok Ragú, 121
Onions
   to chop, 245
   to peel, 245
Oriental dishes, see Chinese
Oranges
   and bananas, sliced, 226
   for dessert, 226
   to prepare, 227
   and scallions, cucumbers, and lettuce salad, 222
Oxtails
   Ökörfarok Ragú, 121
   Ragoût, 193

Peaches with raspberry sauce, 226
Pears
   for dessert, 226
   in Red Wine, 228
Peking Beef Stew
   Stewed Shin Beef, Peking Style, 64
Persian
   Lamb and Bean Khoreshe, 88
   Yoghurt Khoreshe, 57
Pickles, Jim Lee's Chinese Sweet and Sour, 218
Pimientos, leftover, 242
Pistou, Soupe au, 196
Plain Old Chicken and Dumplings, 166
Pork
   cuts for stew, 245
   Lion's Head, 100
   Maiale Affogato, 163
   Stew, Brussels, 93
   Sweet and Pungent, 98
   Szekely Gulyàs, 95
Portuguese Tripe, 189
Potatoes, Zesty New, 217
Pot-au-Feu, 135

Prosciutto, 202
Puchero Criolla, 145
Pumpkin
    Carbonada Criolla, 59

Rabbit
    Lapin aux Prunes, 115
Ragoût de Boeuf Bordelais, 44
Ratatouille I, 124; II, 126
Recipes
    expanding of, 236
    reducing of, 236
Red Cabbage, 217
    and Apple, 216
Red snapper
    in Bouillabaisse, 176
Reheating stew, 245
Rhubarb and Strawberries, Stewed,
    228
Rinsing the pan, 235
Rice
    Lamb Pilaf, 85
    Risotto, 214
    Saffron, 214
Risotto, 214
Russian
    Solianka, 185
    Beef Borscht, 141

Saffron Rice, 214
Sailors' Stew, 118
Salad dressings
    French, 224
    Sauce Vinaigrette, 224
Salads
    beets and endive, 222
    Boston lettuce, Feta cheese, and
        black olives, 222
    endive and watercress, 222
    cucumbers with Sour Cream Dress-
        ing, 223
    garbanzo beans, kidney beans, green
        pepper, onion, and lettuce, 223
    oranges, scallions, cucumbers, and
        lettuce, 222
    raw mushrooms and parsley, 223
    spinach and bacon, 223
    tomatoes and fresh basil, 223
Salmon
    smoked, as appetizer, 205
    Solianka, 185

Sauce Vinaigrette, 223
Sauces for shrimp, 210–11
Sauerkraut
    Szekely Gulyàs, 94
Scallops, see Shrimp Chartreuse
Sea bass
    in Bouillabaisse, 176
    in Sailors' Stew, 118
Seafare Stew, 187
Sea perch
    in Bouillabaisse, 176
Seasoning, to correct, 245–46
Seviche, 207
Shellfish
    in Bouillabaisse, 176
    Seafare Stew, 187
    see also Clams, Crabmeat, and
        Shrimp
Sherbets, 230
Sherry, to flame, 211
Shin Beef, Peking Style, Stewed, 64
Short-Rib Stew, Beef, 33
Shrimp
    in Bouillabaisse, 176
    Chartreuse, 212
    Cold, 209
    Creole Jambalaya, 183
    Flaming, 211
Simmering, 247–48
Sole
    in Bouillabaisse, 176
Soufflé on Toast, Mock, 202
Soupe au Pistou, 196
Sour Cream
    Beef with, 39
    Beef Stroganoff, 41
    Chicken Paprikash, 113
    Russian Beef Borscht, 140
    Szekely Gulyàs, 95
    Veal Paprikash, 69
Sour Cream and Dill Sauce, 211
    cucumbers with, 223
South American beef stew
    Carbonada Criolla, 59
    Puchero Criolla, 145
Spanish
    Ternera al Jerez, 73
Spinach and bacon salad, 223
Squid
    Sailors' Stew, 118

Stew
    cooling, 236
    correcting seasoning, 246–47
    cuts of meat for, 242–44
    fixing up, 238–40
    freezing, 240–41
    frozen, 241
    reheating, 246
    to simmer, 247–48
    timing the cooking, 249
Stewed Shin Beef, Peking Style, 64
Stock, 248
Stifado, 55
Strawberries
    for dessert, 225, 226
    Fruit Compote, 228
    Stewed Rhubarb and, 229
Stufatino, 71
Sweet and Pungent Pork, 98
Sweet and Sour Meatball Stew, 148
Szekely Gulyàs, 95

Tequila
    Margarita Cocktail, 62
Ternera al Jerez, 73
Timing, 249
Tomato(es)
    in Chicken Cacciatore, 111
    and fresh basil, 223
    in Mediterranean Chicken, 108
    paste, leftover, 242
    in Ratatouille I, 124; II, 126
Transylvanian pork goulash
    Szekely Gulyàs, 95
Tripe, Portuguese, 189

Veal
    Blanquette de Veau, 154
    cuts for stew, 245
    Etuvée de Veau au Vin Blanc, 67
    Lemon, 152
    Paprikash, 69
    Stufatino, 71
    Ternera al Jerez, 73
Vegetable combinations, raw, 201
Viennese style goulash
    Wienersaft Gulyàs, 143

Watt, Alexander, 79
White-Bean Casserole, 215

Whiting
    in Bouillabaisse, 176
Wienersaft Gulyàs, 143

Yoghurt Khoreshe, 57

Zesty New Potatoes, 217
Zucchini
    in Ratatouille I, 124; II, 126

69 70 71 72 73 10 9 8 7 6 5 4 3 2 1

...a pile of peeled cherry tomatoes, with ripe olives and coarsely chopped green pepper. The tomatoes can be skinned easily if they are dipped for a moment in boiling water....

...spirals of lemon rind, with cherry tomatoes, and finely chopped fresh parsley.... Coarsely chopped pimientos can be used for the red accent instead of tomatoes....

...on a creamy stew, colored with a little yellow food coloring a sprinkling of finely chopped pimientos...and parsley...

...strips of lightly sautéed green pepper...with ripe olives and chopped pimientos....

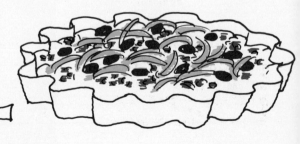